Your Secret Servant

*Fix and Freeze
Hors d'Oeuvres
For Easy
Entertaining*

ANN REED
MARILYN PFALTZ

Designer
Gunnard Faulk

CHARLES SCRIBNER'S SONS

New York

To the MEN IN OUR LIVES . . .

FOREWORD

The authors of "Your Secret Servant" have truly performed a service with their book. The preparation of hors d'oeuvres and canapés receives the fullest treatment between these covers and, added to the fascinating variety, is the invaluable information of how to freeze and defrost each taste delight.

The easy-to-understand instructions also recommend this book to everyone from a beginner in the kitchen to the well-experienced.

"Your Secret Servant" will prove to be your own secret of successful entertaining!

Rebecca Caruba
Author of "Cooking
with Wine and Spirits"

TABLE OF CONTENTS

Foreword   iv

Introduction   vi

Mostly about Freezing   vii

CANAPÉS   1

General Directions for Canapé Preparation   2
     cold
     hot

Flavored Butters   7

Roll-ups   15

Wrap-ups   21

DIPS AND SPREADS   25
     cold
     hot

PASTRY   39

PÂTÉS   65

STORABLES   71

GENERAL HORS D'OEUVRE SELECTION   78
     Cheese   79
     Meat   89
     Fish   99

Abbreviations and Equivalents   110

Index   111

INTRODUCTION

Every hostess dreams of opening the door at her guests' arrival elegantly groomed and prepared to serve a gourmet meal from canapé to nuts. No one should ever know or guess how inelegant she looked that morning standing elbow-deep in pots and dishes wondering why she ever invited anyone in the first place.

The food that greets the guests makes the first impression. It is the food worth laboring over. The hors d'oeuvre are the first bite of food which pass the guests' lips and will tip them off as to what to expect from the kitchen. If the hors d'oeuvre are superb, three drinks later you can serve canned mulligan stew and your guests will remember it as ambrosia.

There is a conspiracy of silence among those who entertain never to reveal the hysterical antics which precede the answering of the doorbell. This cookbook is going to break this conspiracy and reveal the true story behind the scenes — how Madame can serve exotic hors d'oeuvre, enticing entrées and delectable desserts while barely disturbing a hair of her coiffure.

The key to the mystery is in the freezer. YOUR SECRET SERVANT silently stores all those carefully prepared pastries, artistically decorated canapés and unusual taste treats. They can be prepared weeks in advance when the hostess-to-be can give extra care and attention to these "first foods."

No hors d'oeuvre is too difficult for a cook to attempt as long as she is unhurried. You needn't counterfeit the goods by buying expensive packages to warm and serve. You can make everything from sizzling pizza to neatly rolled crêpes and place them in the care of YOUR SECRET SERVANT.

MOSTLY ABOUT FREEZING

Fixing and freezing hors d'oeuvre is fun — not a chore. This book does not pretend to be an elaborate freezer manual. For the intricacies of the art of freezing, there are many complete books available. All YOUR SECRET SERVANT recipes are easily and successfully frozen by following simple directions listed below.

Freeze in Sealed Container. Place the food in a plastic container, leaving about 1″ headspace at the top, and cover tightly with a lid or foil. A lid should be taped on. The container may be wrapped entirely in foil or encased in a tied or taped plastic bag to insure against freezer burn.

To serve: defrost either overnight in the refrigerator or at room temperature for about 2 hours. Anything to be served hot can be slightly thawed for easy removal from the container and then placed directly in the chafing dish or other heated server.

Freeze Uncovered on Trays. Spread the prepared hors d'oeuvre on a cookie sheet, tray or other flat surface and pop in the freezer for an hour or so to quick freeze. Transfer the frozen hors d'oeuvre to a plastic bag which should be securely tied or taped. The bag is a welcome space saver. Because the hors d'oeuvre have been frozen separately, they will not stick together.

To serve: separate and spread hors d'oeuvre on a flat surface so they will not stick together as they defrost. Those that are to be baked or broiled can be placed in the oven directly from the freezer.

Freeze in Layered Trays. Make trays out of heavy duty aluminum foil wrapped around a piece of cardboard or use the aluminum trays salvaged from frozen dinners and store-bought rolls. Place an extra large piece of foil under the first "tray" to use in wrapping the entire package later on. Fill each tray with hors d'oeuvre, placing a sheet of wax paper between each layer. Fold the bottom sheet of foil around all the layers and seal securely. A large plastic bag can be used for extra protection.

All recipes in the book have been tested to freeze for at least three weeks, unless otherwise specified. Label each item with freezing date for easy reference. Each recipe has its own complete freezing directions as well.

Simple isn't it? A minimum of materials, a few easy instructions and you have a SECRET SERVANT ready to serve a gourmet's feast.

CANAPÉS

A canapé is a bite-sized, open-faced sandwich — served hot or cold — imaginatively decorated to please the eye and tempt the palate. Canapés are essentially combinations of breads and spreads. This simple hors d'oeuvre preparation permits you to invent infinite varieties of tastes and decorations with complete confidence for success. The key to producing a spectacular array of canapé platters is *time*. Freezing gives you this time.

Canapés must be frozen before the bread has lost its freshness. The fillings should be made in advance and the bread bases prepared and kept moist under a damp cloth. Select a filling and spread on bread bases. As each variety is completed, these canapés should be wrapped carefully in foil and frozen.

The canapés should be removed from the freezer just barely ½ *hour before serving,* to insure freshness. The small quantity of bread and filling takes little time to defrost. Decorate the canapés with Picasso-like abandon, using a wide variety of garnishes. The prettier they look the better they taste.

This chapter also includes recipes for "Roll-ups" and "Wrap-ups" which are not strictly definable as canapés. However, these hors d'oeuvre are quickly and easily prepared and frozen. They help greatly to expand your regular canapé selection. A well-stocked SECRET SERVANT makes entertaining almost effortless.

GENERAL DIRECTIONS FOR
CANAPÉ PREPARATION

BREAD BASES: Use finely textured bread for best results. Cut unsliced loaf lengthwise into about $\frac{1}{3}''$ slices. Do not use crusts. Use either a sharp knife or a variety of cookie cutters and cut out rounds, triangles, squares or other fancy bite-sized shapes. A bread base which is to be used for a hot canapé should be toasted on one side, the filling placed on the untoasted side, and then frozen.

FLAVORED BUTTERS: The bread bases may be spread with plain butter; a moist filling would make the bread soggy. Flavored butters add an extra zip to the taste and may be used alone or in combination with the spreads.

GARNISHES: The garnishes must be fresh and perky looking. They should be placed on the canapés just before serving. Some garnishes that can be successfully frozen are: small slices of lobster, crab claw bites, sliced turkey, ham or tongue, whole baby shrimp, chopped olive, sieved egg yolk, minced parsley or chives, and chopped nuts. With hot canapés, fresh garnishes such as parsley and watercress must be added after baking.

TO FREEZE: Place the canapés uncovered on a tray or cookie sheet in the freezer. Transfer frozen canapés to a plastic bag for easier freezer storage. The bag should be securely sealed.

TO SERVE: The cold canapés should be spread on a tray and defrosted just before serving. They will taste fresh and moist. Allow about $\frac{1}{2}$ hour for defrosting. Be sure to keep the canapes covered with foil or plastic wrap until serving to prevent dryness. The hot canapés may be heated in an oven directly from the freezer. There is no magic oven temperature. It may vary, depending on what is roasting or baking for dinner.

COLD CANAPÉ SPREADS

General Directions: Combine all ingredients thoroughly. Pile the spread on a prepared canapé base. Follow instructions for preparing canapé bases and for freezing and garnishing finished canapés that are given in the introduction of this chapter. Unless otherwise indicated, the recipes require 16 to 18 bread rounds which can be made from 4 to 5 standard-size bread slices. All canapé spreads may be halved or doubled.

BACON

4 slices bacon
1 3-oz. pkg. cream cheese, softened
2 tbsp. mustard sauce
1 tbsp. minced onion

Fry bacon until crisp. Drain on absorbent paper. Crumble bacon and mix with other ingredients. Spread on prepared canapé bases.

CARROT

1 3-oz. pkg. cream cheese, softened
1 small grated carrot
1 small grated onion
1 tsp. Worcestershire sauce
⅛ tsp. salt
    dash of cayenne pepper

Thoroughly mix all ingredients and spread on prepared canapé rounds. *After* defrosting, garnish with a piece of parsley.

CAVIAR

2 ounces blue cheese
1½ tbsp. butter, softened
2 tsp. sour cream
8 tbsp. caviar (black)
¼ cup lemon juice

Thoroughly blend cheese, butter and sour cream. Spread on prepared canapé bases. Top each canapé with a dab of caviar and a few drops of lemon juice.

CHEESE-PICKLE

⅓ cup grated cheddar cheese
2 tbsp. sweet pickle relish
  tiny gherkin pickles

Combine cheese and relish and spread on prepared canapé bases. Garnish with thin slices of tiny gherkin pickle.

CHICKEN LIVER

⅓ cup minced chicken livers
2 tbsp. minced, fried bacon
  dash of Tabasco sauce
1½ tsp. lemon juice

Combine the ingredients thoroughly, making sure spread is moist. Add more lemon juice if needed. *After* defrosting, garnish with a touch of parsley green. Rye bread rounds are good with this spread.

CRABMEAT-HORSERADISH

½ cup minced crabmeat
1 tsp. light cream
1¼ tbsp. horseradish

Thoroughly combine ingredients and allow to stand for 15 minutes to permit flavors to blend before spreading.

CURRIED CHEESE

1 3-oz. pkg. cream cheese, softened
10 minced ripe olives
½ tsp. curry powder
1 tsp. chopped chives

Garnish with a ½ slice of ripe olive.

DRIED BEEF-CHEESE

⅓ cup minced dried beef
2 tbsp. grated cheddar cheese
mayonnaise to moisten

Combine beef and cheese, adding enough mayonnaise to make a spread.

HAM-CHEESE

⅓ cup grated cheddar cheese
3 tbsp. deviled ham
¼ tsp. Worcestershire sauce
dash of Tabasco sauce
2 tbsp. heavy cream

Add more or less cream as needed to make a spread of the ingredients. This spread goes well with rye bread.

HAM-CHUTNEY

¼ cup minced chutney
¼ cup minced ham
1 3-oz. pkg. cream cheese, softened

Slightly drain chutney before mixing with ham and cheese.

HAM-PINEAPPLE

  ½ cup minced cooked ham or chicken
  2 tbsp. chopped almonds
  2 tbsp. crushed pineapple, drained
    mayonnaise to moisten

Combine ham and almonds in blender. Add pineapple and a touch of mayonnaise, if necessary, to moisten for spreading. *After* defrosting, garnish with a piece of toasted almond. Yield: 28 canapés.

LIVERWURST

  ½ cup mashed liverwurst
  2 tbsp. ketchup or chili sauce
    tiny gherkin pickles

Garnish with a slice of pickle. This spread goes well with rye bread or crackers.

LOBSTER

  ½ cup minced lobster
  2 tsp. lime juice
  2 tsp. minced chives
    salt and pepper to taste
    mayonnaise to moisten

Use a touch of mayonnaise if necessary to moisten for spreading.

PIMIENTO-ANCHOVY

Cover bread rounds with a flavored butter of your choice. Cut piece of pimiento the size of the bread base. Place pimiento on bread and cover with a lattice work of thinly sliced anchovy fillets.

ROQUEFORT-SOUR CREAM

⅓ cup crumbled Roquefort cheese
1½ tbsp. butter
1 tbsp. sour cream
½ cup minced ripe olives
dash of Tabasco sauce

Combine cheese, butter, sour cream, and olives. *After* defrosting, top each canapé with an additional thin slice of olive.

SARDINE-BEET

½ cup mashed sardines
1½ tbsp. mayonnaise
2 tbsp. chili sauce
3 tbsp. minced pickled beets

Drain sardines before combining ingredients. Yield: 28 canapés.

FLAVORED BUTTERS

General Directions: Combine all ingredients thoroughly. Spread the flavored butter on white bread rounds, melba toast, rye or pumpernickle rounds or a favorite cracker. All recipes may be easily halved or doubled. Read freezing and serving directions on preceding pages.

CAVIAR BUTTER

¼ cup butter, softened
1 3-oz. pkg. cream cheese, softened
3 tbsp. black caviar to garnish

Top each canapé with ½ teaspoon of the caviar. Yield: ½ cup.

CHIVE BUTTER

¼ cup butter, softened
¼ cup minced chives or minced scallions
   dash Worcestershire sauce
   dash of Tabasco sauce

Garnish with bits of seafood. Yield: ⅓ cup.

CURRY BUTTER

½ cup butter, softened
2 minced scallions
1½ tbsp. curry powder

Garnish with minced chicken, bits of seafood or slices of olive. Yield: ½ cup.

HERB-WINE BUTTER

2 tbsp. crushed dried herb (thyme or basil or tarragon)
½ cup white wine or lemon juice
½ cup butter, softened

Soak dried herbs in wine or lemon juice and thoroughly mix in the butter. Yield: ½ cup.

HORSERADISH BUTTER

⅓ cup butter, softened
3 tbsp. horseradish
15-20 thin strips of ham

Garnish with thin strips of ham. Yield: ½ cup.

MUSHROOM BUTTER

½ cup butter, softened
½ cup ground raw mushrooms
   salt and pepper to taste

Garnish with small slices of raw mushrooms. Yield:
¾ cup.

OLIVE BUTTER

¼ cup butter, softened
3 tbsp. minced green or ripe olives

Garnish with small slices of olive. Yield: ⅓ cup.

PARMESAN BUTTER

½ cup butter, softened
¼ cup Parmesan cheese
½ tsp. lemon juice
½ tsp. grated onion

This butter goes well on melba toast rounds. Yield:
½ cup.

POPPY OR CARAWAY SEED BUTTER

¼ cup butter, softened
¼ cup ground poppy or caraway seed

This butter is best on rye or pumpernickle base.
Yield: ½ cup.

SARDINE OR SHRIMP BUTTER

¼ cup butter, softened
¼ cup mashed sardines or canned shrimp
   juice of ½ lemon

This butter is best on rye or pumpernickle base.
Yield: ½ cup.

HOT CANAPÉ SPREADS

General Directions: Thoroughly mix all the ingredients. Spread a small amount of the mixture on a prepared canapé base. Follow the instructions given in the introduction of this chapter for preparing canapé bases and freezing and garnishing the finished canapés. To serve: remove frozen canapés from freezer, place on a cookie sheet and bake as directed.

BAKED BEANS

½ cup canned seasoned baked beans, mashed and drained
2 frankfurters, sliced into 12 slices each
24 small squares of medium mild cheese, thinly sliced
24 pumpernickle bread rounds

Spread a teaspoonful of the baked beans on the untoasted side of the bread round. Add a thin slice of frankfurter and a small slice of cheese. Freeze as directed. To serve: bake in 400° oven for about 5 minutes. Yield: 24 canapés.

CHICKEN

½ cup cooked ground chicken
2 tbsp. butter, softened
2 tbsp. pitted ripe olives, finely chopped
½ tsp. onion salt
28 ripe olive slices
28 white bread rounds

Mix all ingredients except the olive slices. Spread on prepared bread rounds and garnish with slices of ripe olives. Freeze as directed. To serve: bake in 400° oven for 5-8 minutes. Yield: 28 canapés.

CLAM

½ cup minced clams
3 tbsp. cream cheese, softened
⅛ tsp. hot pepper sauce
24 white bread rounds
2 strips bacon, cooked and crumbled

Mix first three ingredients and spread on prepared bread rounds. Garnish each with a sprinkling of crumbled bacon. Freeze as directed. To serve: bake in 400° oven for 5-8 minutes. Yield: 24 canapés.

CORNED BEEF

½ cup chopped corned beef
¼ cup Cheese Whiz spread
½ tsp. Worcestershire sauce
24 rye bread rounds
24 olive slices

Combine the corned beef, cheese and Worcestershire sauce. If necessary, add more cheese to make a better spreading consistency. Spread mixture on prepared bread rounds and freeze as directed. To serve: bake in 400° oven for 5 minutes and garnish after heating with an olive slice. Yield: 24 canapés.

CRABMEAT

⅔ cup crabmeat (3¾-oz. can), picked over,
   drained and mashed.
1 tsp. lemon juice
2 ounces (¼ cup) cream cheese, softened
2 tsp. Madeira Wine
1 tsp. onion juice
   salt and pepper to taste
32 white bread rounds

Combine all ingredients and spread on prepared bread rounds. Freeze as directed. To serve: bake in 400° oven for 5-8 minutes until piping hot. Yield: 32 canapés.

HAM-CHUTNEY

    ½ cup cooked ground ham
    ¼ cup chutney
    3 tbsp. salad dressing (not mayonnaise)
    26 rye bread rounds
    ⅓ cup Parmesan cheese

Mix the ham, chutney and salad dressing to a spreading consistency. Spread on prepared bread rounds and sprinkle each with a small amount of Parmesan cheese. Freeze as directed. To serve: bake in 400° oven for 5 minutes. Yield: 26 canapés.

HAM-PINEAPPLE

    24 bread rounds
    ⅓ cup sharp mustard
    24 thin slices ham
    24 pineapple chunks
    24 slices of cheese

Spread the untoasted side of the bread round with mustard. Add slice of ham, piece of pineapple and piece of cheese. Spear with a toothpick. Freeze as directed. To serve: bake in 400° oven for 5-8 minutes until cheese melts. Yield: 24 canapés.

ROAST BEEF

    ½ cup roast beef, cooked and ground
    2 tbsp. minced onion
    4 drops of Tabasco sauce
    ¼ cup ketchup
    16 white bread rounds
    2 strips minced raw bacon

Combine all ingredients except the bacon. If necessary, add more ketchup to make mixture spread easily. Spread on prepared bread rounds and garnish with bits of raw bacon. Freeze as directed. To serve: broil 3-5 minutes until bacon is crisp. Yield: 16 canapés.

SARDINE

1 4-oz. tin sardines, well drained
   dash of Worcestershire sauce
1-2 tbsp. salad dressing
24 white bread rounds

Mash sardines with a dash of Worcestershire sauce and enough salad dressing to make a paste. Spread on prepared bread rounds and freeze as directed. To serve: bake in 400° oven for 5-8 minutes until lightly brown. Garnish with watercress or parsley. Yield: 24 canapés.

TUNA

1 6½-oz. can tuna, well drained
¼ tsp. Worcestershire sauce
¼ tsp. salt
   dash of cayenne pepper
¼ cup mayonnaise
24 white bread rounds

Flake tuna and thoroughly combine with all other ingredients. Spread on prepared bread rounds and freeze as directed. To serve: bake in 400° oven for 5 minutes until brown. Yield: 24 canapés.

WATER CHESTNUT-CREAM CHEESE

¼ cup minced water chestnuts
1 3-oz. pkg. cream cheese, softened
½ tsp. Worcestershire sauce
16 white bread rounds

Mix all ingredients together and spread on prepared bread rounds. Freeze as directed. To serve: bake in 400° oven for 3-5 minutes and garnish with an olive slice or a pickled beet slice. Yield: 16 canapés.

SHRIMP TOAST

¼-½ lb. raw shrimp, deveined
4-6 water chestnuts
1 slightly beaten egg
1 tsp. salt
½ tsp. sugar
2 tsp. minced ginger root
2 tbsp. chopped scallions
1 tsp. sherry wine
1 tbsp. cornstarch
6 slices *firm* white bread
peanut oil for deep frying

Mince shrimp and water chestnuts. Thoroughly combine first nine ingredients. Remove crusts from bread (which should be at least 2 days old — fresh bread will absorb too much oil) and cut each piece into 4 triangles. Spread shrimp mixture on one side of bread triangle.

Pour oil into saucepan until 2″ deep and heat for frying. Cook triangles, 2 or 3 at a time, placing the shrimp side down first. When lightly browned, turn and cook until toast is crisp. Do not overcook, as they also brown in second heating. Use a spatula to lower the toast into the hot oil. Drain very well on absorbent paper.

To freeze: place toasts in layered trays and wrap securely in foil. To serve: place on baking sheet and heat in 400° even for 10-12 minutes or until sizzling hot. Drain on absorbent paper. Yield: 24 pieces.

****Chinese ancestry.

ROLL-UPS
(Hot)

General Directions: Remove crusts from slices of bread and roll each piece flat with a rolling pin. Use finely textured bread so that the fillings will not make the bread too soft. A half-frozen sandwich loaf may be very thinly sliced with a sharp knife, and rolled flat to make the extra delicate roll-ups. Smoothly spread filling on bread and roll like a jelly roll. Brush with melted butter. Place seam side down on a cookie sheet and freeze uncovered. Transfer frozen rolls to a plastic bag for freezer storage. To serve: remove the roll-ups from the freezer. Cut them crosswise into 3 pieces. Bake on a cookie sheet at 400° for 10-15 minutes until brown.

ANCHOVY

2 3-oz. pkg. cream cheese, softened
1 2-oz. can anchovy fillets, drained and minced
3 tbsp. chopped pimiento olives
2 tbsp. sour cream
16 slices white bread
½ cup melted butter

Thoroughly combine all ingredients, except the butter, and spread on prepared bread slices. Roll as directed and brush rolls with melted butter. Freeze and bake as directed. Yield: 48 roll-ups.

ASPARAGUS AND CHEESE

      20 spears cooked asparagus
      20 slices white bread
       3 cups grated sharp cheddar cheese
           juice of 1 lemon
     ½ cup melted butter

Place an asparagus spear across one end of the prepared bread slice and generously sprinkle with grated cheese. Roll like a jelly roll. Add the lemon juice to the melted butter and brush each roll with the lemon butter. Freeze as directed. To serve: cut each roll in 3 pieces before baking. Yield: 60 roll-ups.

MUSHROOM

       1 minced large onion
     1½ cups minced fresh mushrooms
       3 tbsp. butter
       2 tbsp. flour
     ½ tsp. basil
     ½ tsp. salt
     ¼ cup sour cream
      12 slices white bread

Sauté onions and mushrooms in butter until onions are transparent. Add flour, seasonings and sour cream. Heat but *do not boil*. Thoroughly combine mixture and cool slightly before spreading on prepared bread slices. Freeze and bake as directed. To serve: brush the rolls with melted butter before baking. Yield: 36 roll-ups.

DEVILED HAM

1 4½-oz. can deviled ham
3 minced sweet pickles
8 white or rye bread slices

Mix the ham and pickles and moisten to spreading consistency with pickle juice. Spread on prepared bread slices. Freeze and bake as directed. Yield: 24 roll-ups.

HAM AND MUSHROOM

1 minced scallion
1 tbsp. butter
¼ lb. minced mushrooms
½ cup fresh bread crumbs
½ tsp. tarragon
½ tsp. chopped parsley
   salt and pepper to taste
4 large slices boiled ham
1 beaten egg
   bread crumbs, extra fine
1 tbsp. oil

Sauté scallions in butter for 1 minute. Add mushrooms and cook slowly for 10 minutes. Stir in fresh bread crumbs, tarragon, parsley, salt and pepper. Cut ham slices crosswise into 1½″ strips — about 6 to a slice. Spread mushroom mixture on ham strips and roll tightly. Brush with egg and dip into the extra fine bread crumbs to coat. Sauté rolls in combination of 1 tablespoon butter and 1 tablespoon oil until golden on all sides. To freeze: place ham rolls, seam side down, on cookie sheet and freeze uncovered. Transfer frozen rolls to plastic bag for freezer storage. To serve: heat frozen rolls in 400° oven for 6-8 minutes. Yield: 24 roll-ups.

****A delectable combination.

LOBSTER

½ lb. lobster meat, fresh or frozen
4 tbsp. butter
¼ lb. pasteurized processed cheese
20 slices white bread

Cut lobster meat into small pieces. Melt butter and cheese and add lobster meat. Spread lobster mixture on each prepared bread slice. Roll and freeze as directed. To serve: brush each roll with melted butter before baking. Yield: 60 roll-ups.

MUSHROOM-NUT

3 4-oz. cans mushrooms, chopped
1 minced large onion
1 tbsp. butter
  salt and pepper to taste
12 slices white bread
2 3-oz. pkg. cream cheese, softened
  melted butter as needed
1 cup finely chopped pecans

Drain and chop mushrooms. Sauté mushrooms and onion in butter until onion is transparent. Season to taste. Spread prepared bread slices with thin layer of cream cheese. Place a teaspoonful of filling on one end of the slice and roll. Dip the roll in melted butter and then in nuts. Freeze and bake as directed. Yield: 36 roll-ups.

PRESTO PIZZA

  4 slices American cheese
  1 small minced green pepper
  ½ lb. salami
  ½ can tomato paste
  ½ tsp. oregano
20 slices white bread
    melted butter

Grind together cheese, pepper and salami. Add the oregano and tomato paste to the mixture. Combine thoroughly. Spread on prepared bread slices and roll like a jelly roll. Freeze and bake as directed. To serve: brush the rolls with melted butter before baking. Yield: 60 roll-ups.

ROLL-UPS
(Cold)

General Directions: These recipes use a thin slice of ham or bologna instead of prepared white bread slices. The filling should be thinly spread on the meat slice. Roll like a jelly roll. Wrap securely in foil and freeze. To serve: defrost slightly, about 15 minutes, and cut into bite-sized pieces. Do not thaw too long or the rolls become too soft to slice easily.

DILL CHEESE

  1 8-oz. pkg. cream cheese, softened
  ½ cup heavy cream
  ½ cup grated cucumber
  1 tsp. dill seed
    garlic salt to taste
12 slices bologna or thinly sliced boiled ham

Thoroughly mix all the ingredients and spread on the ham slices. Freeze as directed. To serve: arrange rolls on a platter in a pinwheel design and decorate with watercress or a garnish of carrot and radish flowers. Yield: about 36 roll-ups.

PICKLE AND HAM

2 3-oz. pkg. cream cheese, softened
1 tbsp. horseradish
2 tbsp. sharp mustard
½ cup sweet pickle relish, well drained
8 thin slices boiled ham

Mix all ingredients. Prepare and freeze as directed. To serve: the roll-ups may be served alone or on warmed crackers. Yield: about 32 roll-ups.

PINEAPPLE AND HAM

2 3-oz. pkg. cream cheese, softened
½ tsp. salt
1 tsp. lemon juice
1 cup minced celery
8 thin slices boiled ham
1 4¾-oz. can crushed pineapple, drained

Mix all ingredients together except the pineapple. Spread the cheese mixture on ham strip and place a scant teaspoon of pineapple at the end of each strip and roll. Freeze and serve as directed. Yield: about 32 roll-ups.

SALAMI CORNUCOPIAS

1 8-oz. pkg. cream cheese, softened
2 tbsp. horseradish
1 4-oz. pkg. salami slices (small size)
parsley for garnishing

Combine cream cheese and horseradish. Place a teaspoon of this mixture on a round of salami and roll like a cornucopia. Secure with a small piece of toothpick if necessary. *After* defrosting, garnish with a sprig of parsley. Yield: 18 roll-ups.

WRAP-UPS

General Directions: These are all individual recipes which are similarly wrapped in a piece of bacon and broiled or deep fat fried. They are quickly made and easily frozen before or after cooking. A bonus for any cocktail table!

ASSORTED BACON WRAP-UPS

artichoke hearts, canned or frozen
watermelon pickle   bacon

Cut both in bite-sized pieces. Wrap each piece in small slice of bacon. Secure with toothpick. Freeze uncovered on tray. Transfer frozen wrap-ups to plastic bag for freezer storage. To serve: broil on drip rack for 5 minutes until bacon is crisp. Drain on absorbent paper.

SWEET-SOUR RUMAKI
(Water Chestnut Wrap-ups)

1 6-oz. can water chestnuts
½ cup vinegar
½ cup liquid from chestnuts
12 strips of bacon, halved
¼ cup brown sugar

Marinate whole chestnuts in vinegar and chestnut liquid for 1 hour. Drain. Spread each ½ slice of bacon lightly with brown sugar. Roll chestnuts in bacon and fasten with toothpicks. Broil on a drip rack for 5 minutes until bacon is crisp. Drain on absorbent paper. Freeze uncovered on a tray. Transfer frozen wrap-ups to a plastic bag for freezer storage. To serve: reheat in 400° oven for 8-10 minutes. Yield: 24 pieces.

****Far Eastern flavor.

FRANKFURTER AND BACON

bacon
American cheese slices
relish
cocktail frankfurters

Make a slit in the frankfurter. Dab the inside with relish and insert a strip of cheese. Wrap securely with a ½ slice of bacon and secure with toothpick. Freeze uncovered on a tray. Transfer frozen wrap-ups to a plastic bag for freezer storage. To serve: broil on drip rack for 5 minutes until bacon is crisp. Drain on absorbent paper.

CHICKEN LIVER RUMAKI

1 tbsp. sherry wine
1 tsp. garlic powder
3 tbsp. soy sauce
1 tsp. horseradish
½ lb. chicken livers
20 button mushroom (canned or fresh)
½ lb. bacon

Make a marinade of sherry, garlic powder, soy sauce and horseradish. Cut chicken livers into bite-sized pieces and marinate for 2-3 hours in the refrigerator. Cut bacon into small strips, wrap around chicken liver and mushroom, and secure with toothpick. Broil on a drip rack for 5 minutes until bacon is crisp. Drain on absorbent paper. Freeze uncovered on a tray. Transfer frozen wrap-ups to a plastic bag for freezer storage. To serve: heat in 400° oven for 8-10 minutes. Yield: about 20 pieces.

DRIED FRUIT

prunes   olives
apricots   bacon
pears

The fruit should be soaked in rum for 24 hours. The prunes must have pits removed and replaced with pitted green olives. Prepare, freeze and serve as directed above.

CHEESE AND BACON

20 slices white bread
3 cups grated processed American cheese
20 slices bacon

Sprinkle prepared bread slice with grated cheese and cut the slice into 3 lengths. Roll up and wrap each roll with ⅓ slice of bacon. Secure with a toothpick and freeze as directed. To serve: *broil* on a drip rack for 10-15 minutes or until bacon is crisp. Yield: 60 wrap-ups.

PEANUT BUTTER WRAP-UP

crustless bread   bacon
peanut butter

Cut each slice of bread into 6 rectangles and spread with peanut butter. Roll and wrap with bacon. Deep fry in about 2″ hot fat for about 3 minutes. Drain on absorbent paper. Freeze uncovered on a tray. Transfer frozen wrap-ups to a plastic bag for freezer storage. To serve: spread frozen wrap-ups on a cookie sheet and heat at 425° for 5-7 minutes until crisp.

****Intriguing taste.

DIPS

Dips are probably the easiest hors d'oeuvre to prepare and serve. Guests can help themselves and you have an opportunity to display all your best bowls and trays. Unfortunately many hostesses neglect to bother with what goes into the bowl. The old reliable dried onion soup mix and sour cream will not impress guests with your culinary imagination and flair.

Dips should be a real taste adventure. Here is an opportunity to give way to the urge to spice and season by intuitition. Just be sure to keep tasting as you go along. Most dips can change to spreads — and spreads can change to dips — by the addition or subtraction of liquid.

Plastic freezer containers, which come in various sizes, are the most convenient way to store dips. These should be labelled with a washable marker. Always note the freezing date. It is easy to defrost dips overnight in the refrigerator before serving. After a slight thawing, hot dips may be emptied directly into a chafing dish or other warmer.

Though relatively quick and easy to prepare, a dip unmade prior to the arrival of your guests can be the straw which breaks a hostess' back. YOUR SECRET SERVANT is the cure for such last minute frenzy. Fix and freeze at leisure.

SPICY DIP FOR CELERY HEARTS

       2 3-oz. pkg. cream cheese, softened
     ½ cup grated cheddar cheese
     ¾ tsp. salt
    1½ tsp. ground tumeric
     ⅓ tsp. ground cumin seed
     ¼ tsp. ground ginger
     ⅛ tsp. ground black pepper
       2 tsp. chopped pimiento
       1 tsp. minced onion
         celery hearts

Thoroughly combine cream and cheddar cheeses. Add the spices, pimiento and onion. Freeze in sealed container. To serve: turn into a bowl and garnish with additional diced pimiento. Place in center of a large serving plate and surround with chilled, crisp celery hearts. Yield: about 2 cups.

****Festive.

TROPICAL DIP

       1 4½-oz. can deviled ham
       1 cup sour cream
     ½ cup chopped nuts (walnuts, pecans, cashews *or* macadamias)
       1 fresh pineapple

Combine the first three ingredients and freeze in sealed container. To serve: defrost dip overnight in refrigerator. For an interesting serving dish use a pineapple which has been cut in half lengthwise. Remove the core and fruit, leaving shell intact. Cut the fruit in small chunks. Fill one shell with the deviled ham mixture. Serve on a platter surrounded by pineapple chunks, bite-sized apple pieces, and/or grapes, with toothpicks for dipping. Yield: 2¼ cups.

****An eyecatcher!

CLASSIC ROQUEFORT DIP

    4 ounces Roquefort cheese
    ½ cup sour cream
    1 8-oz. pkg. cream cheese, softened
    1 tbsp. minced onion
    7 drops of Tabasco sauce
    1 tbsp. Worcestershire sauce

Mix ingredients. Freeze in sealed container. To serve: defrost overnight in refrigerator. Serve with chips, crackers, or party rye. Yield: about 2 cups.

CHEESE-LAMB DIP

    1 small jar baby food lamb (or beef)
    ½ pt. cottage cheese
    2 tbsp. ketchup
    2 tbsp. minced onion
      salt and pepper to taste

Blend ingredients until well mixed. Freeze in sealed container. To serve: defrost in refrigerator overnight and garnish with parsley, olives or pimiento and serve with crackers or chips. Yield: 2 cups.

BAKED BEAN DIP

    1 lb. can baked beans, mashed
    2 tbsp. minced onion
    ¼ cup minced dill pickle
    1 tbsp. chili powder
    2 minced hard-boiled eggs
    2 tsp. lemon juice
      salt and pepper to taste

Blend ingredients until well mixed. Freeze in sealed container. To serve: defrost overnight in refrigerator and serve with crackers or party rye bread. Yield: about 2 cups.

CRUNCHY DIP

    6 ounces shredded dried beef
    1 pt. sour cream
    1 tsp. chili powder
    ½ cup slivered almonds
    1 tsp. ketchup

Mix all ingredients together. Reserve some of the almonds as a garnish for the dip. Freeze in sealed container. To serve: defrost overnight in the refrigerator and serve with crackers or chips. Yield: about 2½ cups.

ORIENTAL DIP

    ½ cup minced scallion
    ½ tsp. cumin seed
    ¼ cup chopped parsley
    2 tsp. chopped crystallized ginger
    2 tbsp. minced water chestnuts
    1 cup cottage cheese
    1 tbsp. mayonnaise
    ⅓ cup heavy cream

Thoroughly combine all ingredients. Freeze in sealed container. To serve: defrost overnight in refrigerator. Serve with raw mushrooms, cauliflower or other raw vegetables as dippers. Yield: about 2 cups.

****Exotic taste.

BLUE CHEESE DIP

    ½ lb. mashed blue cheese
    1 tbsp. chili sauce
    ¼ cup mayonnaise
    ¼ cup minced onion
    ½ cup minced parsley

Blend all the ingredients until smooth. Freeze in sealed container. To serve: defrost overnight in refrigerator. Garnish bowl with parsley and serve with chips or crackers. Yield: about 2 cups.

SMOKED OYSTER DIP

    1 3-oz. pkg. cream cheese, softened
    ½ cup sour cream
    1 3-oz. can smoked oysters, drained and chopped
    ½ cup minced ripe olives
    1 tsp. grated onion

Thoroughly blend all the ingredients. Freeze in a sealed container. To serve: defrost overnight in refrigerator. Garnish serving bowl with sliced ripe olives and serve with chips or crackers. Yield: about 2 cups.

****Everyone's favorite.

TUNA DIP

    2 4½-oz. cans tuna, flaked
    2 stalks minced celery
    4 tbsp. minced onion
    2 tsp. chervil
      salt and pepper to taste
    1½ tbsp. curry powder
    1 3-oz. pkg. cream cheese, softened
    ½ cup sour cream

Blend all ingredients until smooth. Freeze in sealed container. To serve: defrost overnight in refrigerator. Serve with crackers or chips. Yield: about 2 cups.

SHRIMP INDIENNE DIP

    1 can frozen shrimp soup, thawed
    1 8-oz. pkg. cream cheese, softened
    ¼ tsp. curry powder
    2 tsp. lemon juice
    1 crushed clove of garlic
    1 4-oz. jar ripe olives, minced

Mix all ingredients and chill at least 2 hours for flavors to blend. Freeze in sealed container. To serve: defrost in refrigerator overnight and serve with assorted chips. Yield: about 3 cups.

SHRIMP DIP

1 8-oz. pkg. cream cheese, softened
1 4½-oz. can shrimp, mashed
¼ tsp. curry powder
2 tbsp. mayonnaise
2 tbsp. chili sauce
1 tbsp. lemon juice

Thoroughly combine all ingredients. Freeze in sealed container. To serve: defrost overnight in refrigerator. Garnish bowl with parsley and a few pieces of shrimp and serve with chips. Yield: about 2 cups.

GUACAMOLE DIP

1 peeled tomato
¼ cup grated onion
2 peeled ripe avocados
1 tsp. chili powder
  salt and pepper to taste
2 tbsp. lemon juice

Mash together the tomato and onion. Use a blender if possible. Add avocado and seasonings and blend well. To freeze: place dip in plastic container with a tight lid. Place some wax paper on the surface of the dip. To serve: defrost overnight in the refrigerator. Arrange platter with raw vegetables or crackers for dipping. Sprinkle lemon juice on top of dip to prevent discoloration. Yield: about 1½ cups.

CAVIAR DIP

1 cup whipping cream
⅓ cup caviar (black)
2 tbsp. minced onion
2 tbsp. mashed liver sausage (optional)

Whip cream until stiff. Mix caviar, onion and sausage together and fold into whipped cream. Freeze in sealed container. To serve: defrost overnight in refrigerator. Garnish with hard-boiled egg slices and serve with melba toast. Yield: about 1½ cups.

NUT-CHEESE DIP

½ cup cottage cheese
1 3-oz. pkg. cream cheese, softened
½ cup sour cream
   dash of Tabasco sauce
   pepper to taste
⅛ tsp. garlic powder
½ cup chopped pecans

Thoroughly combine all ingredients and freeze in sealed container. To serve: defrost overnight in the refrigerator and serve with chips. Yield: about 2 cups.

CLAM DIP

1 8-oz. pkg. cream cheese, softened
1 10½-oz. can clams, drained and minced
1 tbsp. Worcestershire sauce
½ tsp. salt
1 tsp. dill seed
   pepper to taste
   dash of Tabasco sauce

Thoroughly combine all ingredients. Freeze in sealed container. To serve: defrost overnight in refrigerator. Serve with favorite chips. Yield: 2¼ cups.

CHEESE-OLIVE DIP

1 8-oz. pkg. cream cheese, softened
8 giant-sized minced ripe olives
2 tsp. grated onion
1 tsp. curry powder
½ cup sour cream

Mix all ingredients until well blended. Freeze in sealed container. To serve: defrost overnight in the refrigerator and serve with assorted chips. Yield: about 2 cups.

CUCUMBER-HAM DIP

    1 cup sour cream
    2 4½-oz. cans deviled ham
    1 grated cucumber
    2 tsp. lemon juice
      dash of Tabasco sauce

Mix all the ingredients until well blended. Freeze in sealed plastic container. To serve: defrost overnight in the refrigerator and serve with assorted chips. Yield: about 2 cups.

CHUTNEY-HAM DIP

    1 4½-oz. can deviled ham
    1 cup sour cream
    ⅓ cup finely chopped chutney

Blend all ingredients thoroughly and freeze in sealed container. To serve: defrost overnight in refrigerator. Serve with nut halves, apple slices, seedless grapes or pineapple chunks, with toothpicks for dipping. Yield: 1⅔ cups.

SOY DIP

    2 cups sour cream
    4 tbsp. soy sauce
    2 tbsp. wine vinegar
    4 drops garlic juice
 1½ tsp. curry powder

Mix all ingredients and chill for several hours so that the flavors blend. Freeze in sealed container. To serve: defrost in refrigerator overnight and serve with artichoke leaves, celery or carrot sticks, shrimp or lobster cubes, or just plain chips. Yield: about 2 cups.

HOT CLAM DIP

1 small minced onion
3 tbsp. butter
¼ lb. American cheese
1 10½-oz. can clams, drained and minced
1 3-oz. pkg. cream cheese
4 tbsp. ketchup
1 tbsp. Worcestershire sauce
½ tsp. cayenne pepper
2 tbsp. sherry or Madeira wine.

Sauté onions in butter until soft. Cut the American cheese into small cubes. Place all ingredients into a double boiler, stirring constantly, until cheeses have melted and mixture is smooth. Cool and freeze in sealed container. To serve: slightly thaw and place in a chafing dish to warm. This can be served as a fondue with small cubes of French bread or with chips. Yield: about 2 cups.

****Clam fondue.

HOT HAM DIP

½ lb. chopped Gruyere cheese
1 4½-oz. can deviled ham
¼ cup ketchup
½ cup bourbon whiskey

Melt the cheese in a double boiler and thoroughly mix in the other ingredients. Cool and freeze in sealed container. To serve: slightly thaw and place in a double boiler or directly in chafing dish to warm. Serve as a fondue with small cubes of French bread or as a fancy hot dip with assorted chips. Yield: about 2 cups.

CHEESE SHRIMP DIP

1 roll or jar processed garlic cheese
1 can frozen shrimp soup
1 small can mushrooms, drained and chopped

Melt all ingredients in the top of a double boiler. Cool. Freeze in sealed container. To serve: defrost in double boiler or chafing dish and serve hot with crackers or cubes of French bread. Yield: about 2 cups.

****A snap to fix.

HOT CURRY DIP

¼ cup chopped onion
¼ cup butter
2 tbsp. flour
3 tbsp. chopped crystallized ginger
2 tbsp. curry powder
2 tsp. salt
1 tsp. sugar
¼ tsp. mint
4 cloves
    dash of cayenne pepper
2 cups milk
⅓ cup shredded coconut
½ cup lime juice
½ cup heavy cream

Sauté onion in butter until soft. Add flour and stir until smooth. Add seasonings. Remove from heat and add milk gradually, stirring until smooth. Simmer 30 minutes. Strain sauce. Cool and freeze in sealed container. To serve: slightly thaw and place in a double boiler or directly in chafing dish to warm. Add coconut, lime juice and heavy cream. Serve hot in chafing dish with shrimp, crisp raw vegetable or apple slices as dippers. Yield: 3½ cups.

CHEESE DIP FOR MEAT

1 lb. grated cheddar cheese
1 cup milk
1 beaten egg
2 tsp. dry mustard
½ tsp. celery seed

Melt cheese in milk, using double boiler. Pour at least half the sauce into the beaten egg and mix. Return the sauce to the pan, add the spices and mix. Cool. Freeze in sealed container. To serve: heat the frozen dip in a chafing dish. Accompany this dip with bite-sized pieces of ham, frankfurters, cooked sausage, bologna, spam, chicken or turkey on toothpicks. Yield: about 3 cups.

CHEDDAR DIP FOR SEAFOOD

¼ cup butter
¼ cup flour
1⅓ cups milk
2 cups grated cheddar cheese
1 tsp. salt
⅔ cup sherry wine
2 slightly beaten eggs

Melt butter and stir in flour. Remove from heat and slowly add milk, stirring until smooth. Return to heat and cook, stirring constantly until smooth and thick. Add cheese, salt and sherry to the sauce and keep stirring until the cheese is melted. Pour at least half the sauce into the beaten eggs and mix. Then return all the sauce to the pan and combine thoroughly. Cool and freeze in a sealed container. To serve: heat in chafing dish. Accompany this dip with bite-sized cubes of shrimp, lobster, scallops, or crab on toothpicks for dipping. Yield: about 3 cups.

****A cheddar fondue.

CRABMEAT DIP

 2 8-oz. pkg. cream cheese
10 ounces picked over crabmeat (canned or frozen)
¼ cup mayonnaise
½ cup sour cream
 2 tsp. dry mustard
 3 tbsp. white wine
1⅓ tbsp. confectioners sugar
 2 tsp. onion juice
   salt to taste

Combine all ingredients in double boiler and heat, mixing until smooth. Cool and freeze in sealed container. To serve: thaw slightly and heat in ovenproof serving dish at 350° until bubbly. Serve with hot crackers. Yield: about 4 cups.

****Dip à la Newburg.

EGGPLANT INDIENNE

1 medium-sized eggplant
  salt
1 slightly beaten egg
1 cup bread crumbs
  fat for frying
1 cup sour cream
½ cup minced chives

Peel eggplant and slice lengthwise. Then slice crosswise into 1″ lengths. Wash and salt the eggplant and set aside for 25 minutes. Rinse off salt and dry eggplant pieces with paper towel. Dip each piece in beaten egg, then bread crumbs and sauté on each side until crisp in preheated frying fat. Drain on absorbent paper.

To freeze: lay side by side on foil and wrap securely. To serve: heat eggplant until bubbly in 375° oven for about 20 minutes. Prepare a dip of 1 cup sour cream and chives to taste. Use toothpicks to serve. Yield: 42 pieces.

FRENCH FRIED MUSHROOMS

2 eggs
1 tsp. salt
  pepper to taste
3 dozen medium-sized mushrooms
  flour
  cracker crumbs
  fat for frying

Beat eggs and season with salt and pepper. Swish mushrooms through flour and dip in eggs. Roll in cracker crumbs and fry in deep, hot fat until golden (about 4 minutes). Drain on absorbent paper. Freeze uncovered on tray. Transfer frozen mushrooms to plastic bag for freezer storage. To serve: separate frozen mushrooms on cookie sheet and heat in 400° oven for 5-10 minutes. Serve on picks for dipping. Yield: 36 mushrooms.

Dill Dip

¾ cup sour cream
¼ cup mayonnaise
1 tbsp. minced dill pickle
1 tsp. chopped capers
1 minced fillet of anchovy

Thoroughly combine all ingredients. Yield: 1 cup.

****A sizzling hot delicacy.

SWISS CHEESE FONDUE

    1 split clove of garlic
    2 cups white wine (Rhine, Riesling or
        Chablis type)
    1 lb. Swiss cheese
    ½ cup flour
        salt and pepper to taste
        few grains nutmeg
    6 tbsp. kirsch or Cognac
    1 loaf day-old French bread

Rub garlic around sides of double boiler or electric skillet. Heat wine until almost boiling. Dredge cheese in flour mixed with salt, pepper and nutmeg. Add several pieces at a time to wine allowing each batch to melt before adding more. Stir constantly with wooden spoon until fondue starts to bubble. When cool, place in sealed container and freeze. To serve: thaw slightly and heat in chafing dish. Add kirsch or Cognac. If fondue becomes too thick, stir in a little preheated wine. To prepare bread: cut lengthwise in fourths and then each length into bite-sized cubes. Use fondue forks or toothpicks to serve. Yield: about 4 cups.

PASTRY

The thought of preparing pastry hors d'oeuvre does not readily occur to most non-professional cooks. The elaborate displays put on by catering establishments and the packaged creations found in the frozen food departments of the nearest market conspire to discourage a do-it-yourself patty shell puff.

Do not be faint of heart! You have a special ally in YOUR SECRET SERVANT. By freezing pastry hors d'oeuvre you may prepare them at a moment when you have the time and are in the mood to undertake something new and different. All of the doughs in the following recipes are easy to prepare.

A word of warning for those who substitute pinches and dashes for teaspoons and tablespoons. Such culinary abandon is not for pastry making. At least half the success of pastry hors d'oeuvre depends on how they look as well as taste. Follow instructions for rolling and shaping as carefully as those for measuring.

Tender loving care in preparation will produce a dazzling array of pastry perfections. A plate of parchment-thin cheese wafers or golden-baked turnovers should *all* be thin and *all* be golden.

CHEESE PASTRIES

American cheese and cream cheese pastry are quick and easy cheese pastry recipes, which can be used to prepare a variety of hors d'oeuvre. The dough can be twisted, braided or cut with cookie cutters as well as shaped into cups, turnovers and pinwheels. The cream cheese pastry is a mild, light pastry which is particularly good to use for turnovers. To freeze: all the pastries should be layered on aluminum trays with wax paper between each layer to prevent the pastries from sticking together. Wrap completely in foil. For extra protection encase in a large plastic bag and seal securely. To serve: place frozen pastries on a cookie sheet and bake as directed. Yield: about 48 hors d'oeuvre.

CREAM CHEESE PASTRY

  1 8-oz. pkg. cream cheese, softened
½ lb. butter or margarine, softened
     dash of salt
  2 cups presifted flour
  1 egg yolk
  2 tsp. cream or milk

Combine the cheese, butter and salt. Work in the flour with a fork or your fingers until a smooth dough is formed. Refrigerate for several hours or overnight before using. Shape as desired and brush the tops of all pastries with the egg yolk beaten with cream. Bake frozen pastries until lightly *golden* in color.

AMERICAN CHEESE PASTRY

2 cups presifted flour
⅔ cup butter or margarine, softened
   dash of salt
1 cup grated American cheese
6-7 tbsp. cold water

Place flour, butter and salt in a bowl. Blend until the particles are the size of coarse meal. Add water slowly until dough holds together. Roll into desired shapes, wrap securely in foil and freeze.

PASTRY VARIATIONS

CHEESE BRAIDS OR TWISTS

Roll either dough to about ⅛″ thickness on floured pastry board or cloth. Cut into finger length strips and twist each strip several times. Freeze uncovered on a tray. Place frozen twists in a plastic bag for freezer storage. To serve: bake frozen twists at 400° for about 15 minutes.

CHEESE COOKIES

Roll either dough to about ⅛″ thickness on a floured pastry board or cloth. Cut in desired shapes and freeze uncovered on trays. Place frozen cookies in a plastic bag for freezer storage. To serve: bake cookies at 400° for about 15 minutes.

CHEESE CUPS

Roll either dough to ⅛″ thickness on a floured surface and cut with 3″ round cutter. Turn up the edges of each round and fit into muffin tins. Prick pastry with a fork and bake at 400° for about 15 minutes. Freeze uncovered on a tray and *carefully* place in a plastic bag for freezer storage. To serve: bake frozen cups in preheated 400° oven for about 5 minutes until hot and then fill with desired filling. They may be served hot or cold.

Filling: cups may be filled with seasoned shrimp, lobster, tuna or chicken salad, mushrooms, caviar or any flavorsome combination.

PASTRY PINWHEELS

Roll either dough into an oblong about ⅛″ thick. Spread with a prepared mixture. Beginning with the long side, roll up firmly. Wrap securely in foil and freeze. To serve: cut crosswise into ⅓″ thick slices and bake at 425° for about 15 minutes.

Suggested Mixtures

Tuna: mix 3 chopped anchovies with 1 can of tuna, 2 tsp. lemon juice, 2 tbsp. tomato paste and ¼ tsp. of Tabasco sauce.

Blue Cheese: mix cream cheese and blue cheese and moisten with cream.

Deviled Ham: moisten 1 can deviled ham with a mild mustard or commercial mustard sauce.

TURNOVERS

Roll the cream cheese dough on a floured surface to about ⅛″ thickness and cut into 3″ round circles. Place a teaspoonful of filling just off center on each circle. Fold dough over filling and press edges to seal. Crimp the edge with floured fork tines. Freeze filled turnovers uncovered on a tray. Place them in a plastic bag for freezer storage. To serve: bake frozen turnovers in 375° oven for 15-20 minutes.

Suggested Fillings

Mushroom

- ½ lb. fresh mushrooms
- 3 tbsp. butter
- 1 minced onion
- 2 tsp. flour
- ½ tsp. salt
  pepper to taste
- 1 tsp. dried dill
- ½ cup sour cream

Wash mushrooms, trim off the toughest stems and chop finely. Sauté onions and mushrooms in the butter until tender. Add flour, salt and pepper. Cook for 1-2 minutes. Remove from heat and stir in sour cream and dill. Cool.

Shrimp

- 2 4½-oz. cans shrimp
- 3 chopped green onions
- 2 tsp. spicy prepared mustard
- ½ tsp. tarragon
  salt to taste
- 6 tbsp. sour cream

Drain and finely chop the shrimp. Thoroughly combine all ingredients.

Spicy Beef

- 1 lb. ground beef
- 3 tbsp. olive oil
- 1 pkg. spaghetti-sauce mix
- 1 minced small onion
- 1 tomato, peeled and chopped
- ½ tsp. salt
- ¼ cup water
- ½ cup grated cheddar cheese
- ¼ cup grated Parmesan cheese

Brown beef in olive oil. Add sauce mix, onion, tomato, salt and water. Cook 10-15 minutes. Remove from heat and stir in the cheeses. Cool.

CHILI-SHRIMP SQUARES

- 1 cup butter or margarine, softened
- 1¾ cups sifted flour
- ½ tsp. salt
- 2 tbsp. minced onion
- 2 tsp. steak sauce
- 1 tsp. chili powder
- 1½ cups canned shrimp
  (2 4½-oz. cans), mashed
- 1 egg yolk
- 1 tsp. milk

Combine butter, flour and salt. The best way to do this is with your fingers. Knead until dough holds together. Thoroughly mix in onion, steak sauce, chili powder, and mashed shrimp. Roll out dough on floured board to about ½″ thickness. Cut into 1½″ squares.

To freeze: place squares uncovered on tray. Transfer frozen squares to plastic bag for freezer storage. To serve: place frozen squares on cookie sheet. Brush with egg yolk, which has been beaten with milk. Bake in 400° oven for 10-12 minutes. Yield: 30 squares.

PEANUT BUTTER BRAIDS

⅓ cup butter, softened
2 3-oz. pkg. cream cheese, softened
½ tsp. salt
1 cup flour
   chunk-style peanut butter
8 slices crisply fried bacon

Pastry: Mix the butter, cream cheese, and salt until well blended. Then gradually work in 1 cup of flour. Pat into a rectangle about 6″ wide. Wrap in wax paper and chill in the refrigerator for at least ½ hour so that the butter can harden and the dough can be more easily handled.

Roll into a long rectangle on a lightly floured board. Cut in half lengthwise. Spread half with chunk-style peanut butter. Crumble the bacon over the peanut butter and smooth over gently with a knife. Cover with other half of dough. Cut crosswise into strips ½″ wide. Twist each strip to make a braid effect and cut in half. They are easier to cut when frozen.

To freeze: place uncovered on a tray. Transfer frozen braids to a plastic bag for freezer storage. To serve: place frozen braids on an ungreased cookie sheet and bake at 375° near top of oven for 15-20 minutes until golden brown. Serve warm. Yield: about 32 braids.

CUMIN SEED WAFERS

¾ cup butter, softened
3 ounces grated sharp cheddar cheese
1 cup sifted flour
2 tsp. cumin seed

Combine butter and cheese until thoroughly blended. Gradually add the flour and cumin seed and mix well. Shape dough into a roll about 1½″ diameter for slicing and baking. To freeze: wrap securely in foil. To serve: defrost for approximately 15 minutes or until the dough will slice easily. Slices should be about ⅓″ thick. Bake in 400° oven for 8-10 minutes. Serve hot. Yield: about 36 wafers.

BLUE CHEESE COOKIES

½ cup butter, softened
1 cup flour
3 ounces blue cheese
1 ounce grated very mild cheddar cheese
  egg white
  paprika
  poppy seeds

Thoroughly mix together the butter, flour and cheeses. Shape dough into a roll of about 1½" diameter for slicing and baking. To freeze: wrap in foil. To serve: defrost for approximately 15 minutes or until dough will slice easily. Cut in ⅓" slices and brush each slice with egg white mixed with paprika. Sprinkle poppy seeds on each, and bake on a greased cookie sheet at 450° for 10 minutes. Yield: about 30 cookies.

****Easy and good.

CHEESE WAFERS

½ cup grated sharp cheddar cheese
5 tbsp. butter, softened
¾ cup sifted flour
½ tsp. salt
  dash of cayenne pepper
¼ tsp. garlic powder
½ tsp. thyme

Thoroughly cream the cheese and butter together. Add remaining ingredients. Shape dough into a roll about 1½" diameter for slicing and baking. To freeze: wrap securely in foil. To serve: defrost for approximately 15 minutes or until dough will slice easily. Slice in ⅓" pieces and bake in 400° oven for 8-10 minutes. Serve hot or cold. Yield: about 36 wafers.

****A snap to fix — guests' favorite.

CURRIED CHEESE COOKIES

1 tsp. flour
1 cup grated mild cheddar cheese
1 tsp. curry powder
1 tsp. garlic salt
2 egg whites
1 tbsp. sherry wine

Mix the flour, cheese and seasonings. Beat egg whites until stiff and fold into the cheese mixture. Gently fold in the wine. Shape into bite-sized balls. Freeze uncovered on a tray. Transfer frozen cookies to a plastic bag for freezer storage. To serve: place frozen cookies on greased cookie sheet and bake at 350° until very puffy for about 25-30 minutes. Raise heat to 450° and bake about 5 minutes until the tops are brown. Yield: 36 cookies.

****Tangy taste.

SESAME CHEESE WAFERS

4 tbsp. sesame seeds
½ lb. well-aged Cheddar cheese, grated
½ cup butter, softened
1 tsp. mustard
¾ tsp. powdered ginger
  salt to taste
1 cup sifted flour

Brown sesame seeds in shallow pan in 350° oven for about 15 minutes. Combine cheese, butter, mustard, ginger and salt. Blend well and add flour and seeds. Shape dough into roll about 1½" diameter for slicing and baking. To freeze: wrap securely in foil. To serve: defrost for approximately 15 minutes or until dough will slice easily. Slices should be about ⅓" thick. Bake in 400° oven for 8-10 minutes. Serve hot. Yield: about 36 wafers.

PARMESAN WAFERS

½ cup butter, softened
½ cup grated Parmesan cheese
1 cup sifted flour
½ tsp. baking powder
½ tsp. salt

Cream butter and blend thoroughly with Parmesan cheese. Sift together flour, baking powder, and salt, before combining with cheese and butter. Shape dough into a roll about 1½″ diameter for slicing and baking. To freeze: wrap securely in foil. To serve: defrost for approximately 15 minutes or until dough will slice easily. Slices should be about ⅓″ thick. Bake in 400° oven for 8-10 minutes. Serve hot. Yield: about 36 wafers.

****Crisp and crunchy.

OLIVE CHEESE BALLS

½ cup butter, softened
2 cups grated sharp cheddar cheese
  (about 6 oz.)
1 cup sifted flour
½ tsp. salt
1 tsp. paprika
1 10½-oz. jar pimiento olives

Cream butter and cheese together until smooth. Gradually add flour, salt and paprika and blend well to make dough. Take 1 teaspoon of dough and completely wrap around each olive. Freeze on flat tray. Transfer frozen balls to a plastic bag for freezer storage. To serve: place frozen olive balls on a cookie sheet and bake 15 minutes in 400° oven. Yield: about 48 olive balls.

For variations: break off enough dough to make a bite-sized ball. Make a hollow in the center and fill with deviled ham, pickled cocktail onion, or a small piece of watermelon pickle. Be sure to seal dough around filling.

****A real favorite.

PIROZHSKI

Pastry

1 cup sour cream
½ cup butter, melted and cooled
2 eggs
1 tsp. baking powder
1 tsp. salt
¾ cup all-purpose flour (or enough to make dough stiff)

Thoroughly combine sour cream, butter and 1 egg. Add baking powder, salt and flour. Chill dough for several hours to stiffen. Roll out dough thinly and cut into circles 2¼" in diameter. Place 1 teaspoon of filling in center of each circle. Fold over and pinch edges to seal. Prick each piece for baking.

Filling

1 lb. ground beef
1 tbsp. butter
1 chopped medium onion
¼ cup beef bouillon
1½ tsp. salt
½ tsp. pepper
2 minced hard-boiled eggs
1 minced green pepper

Brown beef in butter with onion and add seasonings. Mix in the hard-boiled eggs and green pepper. Moisten with bouillon.

To freeze: place uncovered on a cookie sheet. Transfer frozen turnovers to a plastic bag for freezer storage. To serve: brush frozen pirozhski with beaten egg and bake in 425° oven for 15 minutes or until lightly brown. Serve hot or cold. Yield: about 80 pirozhski.

****Russian turnovers.

COCKTAIL CRÊPES

Batter

1 cup flour
¼ tsp. salt
2 eggs
1 cup milk (or ½ milk and ½ chicken broth)

Combine the dry ingredients. Beat eggs lightly; then sift dry ingredients over top and beat until smooth. Stir in milk. Let stand for an hour or so to blend flavors. Use 6″ diameter iron skillet, very lightly greased. To test proper temperature, sprinkle a few drops of water on pan and, if they bounce, all is ready.

Pour a large mixing spoonful (approximately 1½ ounces) of batter into pan. Cook about 1 minute per side, making sure the crêpe is set and golden on either side. Remember to lightly grease pan before each batch. Stack crêpes with wax paper between layers and prepare the filling.

Crêpe Assembly

Spread a heaping tablespoon of filling on a crêpe and roll tightly. To freeze: place on trays and wrap securely in foil. To serve: cut each crêpe in thirds and warm in 400° oven for about 10 minutes. Yield: about 90 crêpes.

CHOICE OF FILLINGS

Cheese Crêpe Sticks

Cut Swiss cheese into small ¼″ thick sticks about 2″ or 3″ long. Roll sticks in crêpes and dip crêpes in egg, slightly beaten, and in fine fresh bread crumbs. Quickly fry crêpes in deep, hot fat. Wrap in foil and freeze. To serve: heat in 400° oven. Yield: 30 crêpes.

Chicken

- 3 tbsp. butter
- 3 tbsp. flour
- ¼ tsp. salt
- dash of cayenne pepper
- 1½ cups milk
- 2 tbsp. cream
- ¼ cup Sauterne wine
- 1 slightly beaten egg yolk
- ¼ lb. sliced fresh mushrooms
- 1½ cups cooked chicken or turkey, chopped
- 4 tbsp. butter for sautéeing

Make a cream sauce by melting 3 tablespoons butter in saucepan over low flame or in top of double boiler and stir in flour, salt and cayenne. Cook until simmering. Add milk, stirring constantly, until sauce thickens. Remove from heat.

Slowly stir mixture of cream, wine, and egg yolk into cream sauce. Cook, still stirring, for 1 minute. Fold in chicken and mushrooms sautéed in 4 tablespoons butter.

Newburg

- 3 tbsp. butter
- 3 tbsp. flour
- ½ tsp. salt
- dash of cayenne pepper
- 1½ cups milk
- 2 tbsp. cream
- ¼ cup sherry wine
- 1 slightly beaten egg yolk
- 5 ounces cooked shrimp
- 7 ounces cooked crabmeat

Make cream sauce as directed in chicken filling. Add cream and sherry to egg yolk and slowly stir into cream sauce. Cook, still stirring, for 1 minute. Fold in chopped, cooked shrimp and crabmeat.

****A gourmet's delight.

SWISS CHEESE PUFFS

½ cup water
¼ tsp. salt
1¼ tbsp. butter
¼ lb. Swiss cheese (or cheddar)
⅔ cup flour
3 eggs

Heat the water, salt and butter in a saucepan until the butter is melted. Add cheese and stir until the mixture is creamy. Add flour all at once and stir vigorously until mixture forms a ball. Add eggs, one at a time, stirring until each egg is absorbed. Drop by teaspoonful onto a lightly greased cookie sheet. Bake at 450° for 10 minutes, then 350° for 10 minutes. Remove from oven and cool. Cut off tops of puffs and fill with chicken or seafood salad.

Chicken Salad Filling

1 cup minced, cooked chicken, (tuna, crab or shrimp)
2 tbsp. minced onion
2 tbsp. minced celery
salt and pepper to taste
1 tsp. minced parsley
1 tbsp. minced pimiento (optional)
2 tbsp. sour cream to moisten

To freeze: Layer puffs on trays with wax paper between the layers and wrap securely in foil. To serve: defrost overnight in refrigerator. Serve either warm or cold. Unfilled puffs may be served as a plain cheese pastry. Yield: about 24 puffs.

****Cocktail cream puffs.

FRITTERS

1½ cups flour
2 tbsp. baking powder
½ tsp. salt
1 egg
½ cup milk
  fat for deep frying

Thoroughly combine all ingredients. Drop by ½ teaspoon into hot deep fat. Fry until golden. Drain on absorbent paper. Freeze uncovered on a cookie sheet. Transfer frozen fritters to a plastic bag for freezer storage. To serve: heat frozen fritters in 400° oven for about 8 minutes until crisp.

For variations, mix one of the following into the batter: ½ cup grated cheese, 1 cup dried minced beef, 1 cup finely chopped peanuts, 1 cup minced onion, 1 cup minced olives, 1 mashed banana, 1 cup minced apple, 1 lb. fried crumbled bacon, 1 cup minced mushrooms or 1 cup minced franks. Freeze and serve as directed above. Yield: about 48 fritters.

Note: plain fritters may be served hot with an accompanying dip of your choice.

Dill Sour Cream Dip

1 cup sour cream
  dill seed
1 tsp. minced onion
  salt and pepper to taste

Combine all ingredients thoroughly. Add as much dill seed as desired.

****Superb.

FILO PASTRY

Any hors d'oeuvre made with this flaky, paper-thin dough brings forth the most lavish praise from guests. It is really not difficult to work with once you become accustomed to handling the strudel-like pastry leaves. Allow an extra half hour the first time to experiment because even the most experienced hands waste some leaves.

You may purchase the pastry leaves in most stores selling gourmet items or specialty shops featuring Greek or Near Eastern foods.

To prepare: keep filo dough frozen until ready to use. Remove from freezer the night before using, and refrigerate. Lay a damp towel on working surface, then a piece of wax paper, the filo sheets, a piece of wax paper and a second damp towel — in that order. This preparation prevents the dough from drying while you work. Carefully remove a sheet of filo and brush with melted sweet butter (an ordinary inexpensive 1" paint brush is quickest and easiest). Cut the sheet into about 7 strips. Double over the end of the strip about ½" and put a teaspoon of filling on the double thickness. Fold first turn in the shape of a triangle and fold over and over as a flag. Work quickly to prevent the sheet from drying.

CHOICE OF FILLINGS

Cheese

1 beaten egg
1 lb. cottage cheese, small curd
¾ cup grated Romano cheese
⅓ lb. crumbled Feta cheese

Combine beaten egg and cheeses. Follow directions for filo dough preparation.

Lamb

½ lb. ground lamb (or beef)
3 tbsp. butter
1 tbsp. tomato sauce
1 tbsp. chopped parsley
¼ tbsp. cinnamon
  salt and pepper to taste

Quickly brown ground lamb in butter. Add tomato sauce, parsley, cinnamon and salt and pepper. Simmer for 5 minutes or until liquid boils down. Follow directions for filo dough preparation.

Spinach and Cheese

1 10-oz. pkg. frozen leaf or 1 lb. fresh spinach
1 minced onion
3 tbsp. olive oil
½ lb. Feta cheese
6 ounces pot cheese
¼ cup chopped parsley
1 tsp. crumbled dill weed
½ tsp. salt
  pepper to taste
3 eggs
⅓ cup corn flake crumbs

Thaw and cut spinach into small pieces with scissors. Drain thoroughly. Sauté onion in heated oil until translucent. Add spinach and simmer until moisture evaporates. Crumble Feta cheese into a bowl and blend in pot cheese, parsley, dill weed, salt and pepper. Beat eggs and combine with cheese mixture. Add spinach and onion and stir in crumbs. Blend thoroughly. Follow directions for filo dough preparation.

Crab

½ cup sour cream
1 tsp. dry mustard
1 tsp. grated onion
1 tbsp. dried kosher-styled dill dip
  or 1 tbsp. plain dill
1 tsp. salt
½ cup Grape-Nuts cereal
1 6½-oz. can minced crabmeat

Combine sour cream, mustard, onion, dill, salt and Grape-Nuts. Add crabmeat, and, if time permits, refrigerate for several hours to allow flavors to blend. Follow directions for filo dough preparation.

Freezing Instructions

To freeze: brush wax paper with melted sweet butter; place canapés separately on buttered wax paper. Brush the tops of all canapés with butter and cover with a second piece of wax paper. To freeze in layers, be sure the canapés are placed on a buttered surface and are themselves buttered before covering. They may be stored in ordinary cardboard boxes or aluminum foil tins and then encased in a plastic bag to seal.

To serve: remove from freezer several hours before baking. Place on cookie sheet and bake in 350° oven for 25-30 minutes or until golden brown. Drain on absorbent paper and serve piping hot.

A box of 40 filo sheets 8½″ x 11″ should make about 240 pieces.

****Takes time, not talent — a piece de resistance!

BACON BISCUITS

⅔ cup milk
2 cups Bisquick
¾ lb. crisply fried bacon

Preheat oven to 425°. Stir milk into Bisquick with a fork. Beat vigorously 15 strokes until dough is stiff. Thoroughly mix in crumbled bacon, reserving about 1 cup for garnishing. Knead dough for 1 minute. Roll out on a lightly floured board to ½″ thickness and cut out biscuits with a small juice glass or small cookie cutter 1½″ in diameter. Press some bacon into top of each biscuit. Wrap securely in foil and freeze. To serve: bake in 375° oven for 15 minutes or until lightly browned. Yield: about 48 biscuits.

CAMEMBERT BISCUITS

¼ cup butter
3 ounces ripe Camembert cheese*
¼ cup grated Swiss cheese
3 eggs
1 tsp. salt
2 cups sifted flour

Cream butter and blend in Camembert (rind included) and Swiss cheese. Add eggs, one at a time, beating well after each addition. Stir in salt and flour. Mix until soft dough is formed. On a lightly floured board, pat dough into a circle 10″ in diameter. Cut into pie-shaped wedges of desired size. (A biscuit cutter also may be used.)

To freeze: wrap in foil. To serve: bake in 350° oven for 20-25 minutes or until just brown and bubbly.

****Goes well with beer.

*Liederkranz or Limburger cheese may be used instead of Camembert.

ONION PIZZA

1 pkg. hot roll mix
1 tbsp. olive oil

Prepare according to package directions for pizza.
Add the tablespoon of oil as you are kneading the
dough. Roll the dough thin enough to line a 11" x 16"
baking pan. Several smaller pans may be used instead
of a single large one.

Filling

3 lb. minced onions
2 minced cloves of garlic
1¼ tsp. salt
½ tsp. pepper
¾ cup olive oil
2 cans anchovy, sliced
1 small can pitted black olives, sliced thinly

Season onions and garlic with salt and pepper and
sauté in oil for 20 minutes. Spread this mixture on
dough. Arrange anchovies in decorative lattice design
on top. Use thinly sliced olives to complete the design.
Bake at 350° for 30 minutes.

To freeze: wrap securely in foil. Cut into squares
while still frozen, leaving design intact. To serve: heat
in 400° oven for about 7 minutes. Place on platter with
design intact and garnish with watercress and parsley.
Yield: about 45 squares.

****Very decorative.

PARTY PIZZA

Pastry

⅓ cup butter or margarine
½ cup corn meal
1½ cups flour
1 tsp. salt
⅓ cup water

Cut butter into mixed dry ingredients with 2 knives or fingers until dough is the consistency of coarse meal. Add water slowly until dough holds together. Knead for a few seconds. Roll until piecrust-thin. Cut with small round cutter or juice glass. Prick rounds and turn up the edges. Bake at 425° for 10 minutes. Set aside to cool and prepare filling.

Filling

olive oil
small can of tomato sauce
Parmesan cheese
basil
oregano
freshly ground pepper
¼ lb. cooked sausage (optional)
small can anchovies
Mozzarella cheese, sliced

Brush olive oil on pastry. Sprinkle with Parmesan. Spoon about 2 teaspoons of tomato sauce on top. Sprinkle with a pinch of basil, oregano and pepper. Top with a small piece of cooked sausage or anchovy, more Parmesan and a generous slice of Mozzarella cheese. Freeze on trays securely wrapped in foil. To serve: broil until cheese is melted and the edges are brown. Yield: about 30 pizza.

****Good cocktail party fare.

QUICHE LORRAINE TARTLETS

Pastry

- ½ cup butter, softened
- ½ tsp. salt
- 1 tsp. sugar
- 1½ cups flour
- ½ cup water
- 1 egg white

Blend butter, salt and sugar into flour with fingers or pastry blender until dough is consistency of coarse meal. Make a well in flour. Add ¼-½ cup water or enough to gather dough into a ball. Wrap and refrigerate for at least 2 hours. Dough can be stored in refrigerator for a week or more. Roll out dough to ⅛″ thickness and cut with 3″ round cutter. Place dough rounds in muffin tins. Prick each pastry with fork and bake in preheated 450° oven for 5 minutes. Brush each pastry with white of egg and prepare filling and custard as directed.

Filling

- 6 bacon strips
- 1 chopped onion
- 1 tbsp. butter
- 1 cup cubed Swiss or Gruyere cheese
- ⅓ cup Parmesan cheese

Cook bacon strips until crisp. Chop and cook onion in butter. Crumble bacon. Place small amount of bacon, onion and cheese into each tartlet.

Custard

- 4 lightly beaten eggs
- 2 cups light cream or 1 cup milk and 1 cup light cream
- ¼ tsp. nutmeg
  dash of cayenne pepper
- ½ tsp. salt

Combine all the above ingredients and pour a little custard over the cheese mixture in each tartlet.

To freeze: place the tartlets on trays and wrap securely in foil. To serve: bake frozen quiches in 450° oven for 15 minutes. Then reduce heat to 350° and bake 45 minutes or until the quiches are puffed and brown and custard is set. To test, insert the tip of a knife. If the custard is ready, the knife should come away clean. Quiches may be served warm.

****An all-time favorite.

DEVILED HAM PINWHEELS

Pastry

1 cup flour
1 tsp. chili powder
¼ cup butter
1 3-oz. snappy cheese roll or cheese pack refill

Combine all ingredients. Using a pastry blender or fingers, mix until dough is crumbly and well blended. One tablespoon of cold water may be used, if needed, to make the dough more workable. Form into a ball and refrigerate for several hours to allow the seasonings to blend.

Filling

1 3¼-oz. can deviled ham
¼ tsp. dry mustard
pepper to taste

Roll pastry on floured board into a rectangular shape approximately 12½″ x 6½″. Spread filling thinly across the dough and roll lengthwise into a pinwheel roll. Wrap securely in foil and freeze. To serve: defrost and slice into ¼″ slices. Place on a cookie sheet and bake in 400° oven for 10-12 minutes until sizzling, crisp. Yield: about 36 pinwheels.

****Mexican flavor.

CHEESE BISCUITS

1 pkg. refrigerated biscuits (sold in a roll)
¼ cup melted butter
½ cup grated cheddar cheese

Cut each biscuit into 4 wedges. Roll each wedge in melted butter; then roll in grated cheese. Bake at 400° for 12 minutes. Freeze uncovered on a tray. Transfer frozen biscuits to a plastic bag for freezer storage. To serve: heat frozen biscuits in hot oven. Yield: 48 biscuits.

****Quickie.

PATTY SHELL PUFFS

1 pkg. frozen patty shells
1½ cups minced cooked chicken, turkey, bacon, shrimp, crab or lobster
1 tbsp. heavy cream
2 tsp. minced onion
1 tsp. tarragon
1 tsp. lemon juice
dash of nutmeg
salt and pepper to taste

Slightly thaw patty shells and roll to ¼″ thickness. Cut each into 6 pieces. Prepare filling by combining above ingredients. Place a teaspoonful of this mixture on each piece of pastry; fold in sides and neatly roll. Freeze uncovered on trays. Transfer frozen puffs to plastic bag for freezer storage. To serve: bake frozen puffs in 450° oven for 10-12 minutes. These puffs may be served hot or cold. Yield: 36 puffs.

****One of our best.

BUCKWHEAT DIPPERS

1 egg
1 cup buckwheat pancake mix
1 cup milk
2 tbsp. melted butter

Beat the egg and stir in remaining ingredients until batter is smooth. Drop batter by the teaspoonful onto a hot griddle. Brown on both sides and set aside to cool. Wrap pancakes in foil to freeze. To serve: heat pancakes still wrapped in foil in a slow oven. Serve warm with dishes of caviar and seasoned sour cream. Yield: about 84 pancakes.

****Cocktail pancakes.

PARMESAN MERINGUES

3 egg whites
¼ tsp. salt
3 ounces freshly grated Parmesan cheese
fat for deep frying

Beat the egg whites until stiff. Fold in the salt and cheese. Drop by teaspoonful into hot, deep fat and fry until golden brown. Use slotted spoon to turn and remove to absorbent paper. Drain thoroughly. Freeze on trays. Transfer frozen meringues to plastic bag for freezer storage. To serve: heat in 375° oven for 5-10 minutes. Yield: about 24 meringues.

****Cheese ambrosia.

PÂTÉS

Any food feature in a woman's magazine picturing an appealing selection of hors d'oeuvre invariably includes an eyecatching pâté. A handsomely garnished pâté is an important element to assure successful entertaining. As a hostess of distinction, you naturally feel compelled to attempt such a creation. There is seldom, if ever, an explanation of how you find the time to put together this delectable appetizer and still have the entrée and dessert ready for dinner.

The answer is simple. All you need do is fix and freeze the pâté days or weeks in advance and store it, carefully sealed, in YOUR SECRET SERVANT. Remember, this exotic fare is really nothing but a seasoned paste made from chicken or other livers.

Many famous restaurants have their own pâté specialties. These include some of the more spectacular of the gastronomic pâté dishes such as foie gras, prepared starting with the goose — not the can.

The recipes in this chapter are *easy* to make and each has a different and distinctive taste. With a little effort, you can adopt some of the following recipes as your own "specialty of the house." Various fish meats have been used, as well as the customary livers.

Pâtés are decorative and should be the center of attention. They can be molded into different shapes, either by hand or by using a metal form. Serve garnished with capers, pimiento, parsley, sliced olives or whatever else your artistic sense desires.

MOCK LIVER PÂTÉ

1 lb. mashed braunschweiger liverwurst
1 8-oz. pkg. cream cheese, softened
¼ cup Cognac
¾ cup minced raw mushrooms
1 crushed clove of garlic
1 tsp. minced parsley
1 tsp. Worcestershire sauce

Combine ingredients. Form a loaf, wrap securely in foil, and freeze. To serve: defrost slowly overnight in the refrigerator. Garnish with raw mushroom slices. Serve with party rye bread or crackers. Yield: 3¼-4 cups.

****Pâté à la SECRET SERVANT.

SHRIMP PÂTÉ

1 lb. raw shrimp, peeled and deveined
2 tbsp. butter
¼ cup butter, softened
1 tsp. hot mustard
　dash of Tabasco sauce
3 tbsp. sherry wine
　juice of 1 lemon *or*
1 tsp. grated lemon peel

Sauté the shrimp in 2 tablespoons of butter over low heat until pale pink (approximately 3-5 minutes). Grind shrimp in blender. Add ¼ cup of softened butter, mustard, Tabasco, sherry and lemon juice. Blend this mixture thoroughly. Freeze in sealed plastic container.

The pâté may be molded in a fish mold. Remove and freeze, taking care not to disturb the shape. To serve: defrost overnight in refrigerator and decorate appropriately with capers for eyes and a slice of pimiento for fish's mouth. Serve with a plain cracker. Yield: about 2½ cups.

****Looks elegantly professional.

LIVER PÂTÉ #1

½ lb. chicken liver
½ lb. calf's liver
½ lb. ground veal
½ cup heavy cream
¼ lb. sweet butter, softened
2 ounces Cognac
salt and pepper to taste

Work the chicken and calf's liver through the medium blade of food grinder and thoroughly mix in ground veal and heavy cream. Place mixture in buttered loaf pan. Stand pan in container of hot water and bake in 325° oven for 3 hours. Remove from oven and cool. Put mixture through a sieve and stir in sweet butter, Cognac, salt and pepper. Beat until pâté is fluffy. Pack the pâté into decorative crocks or plastic containers and cover securely to refrigerate or freeze.

To serve: defrost overnight in refrigerator and serve at room temperature. *After* defrosting, garnish with fresh parsley. Yield: 2½ cups.

LIVER PÂTÉ #2

1 chopped small onion
4 tbsp. butter
1 lb. chicken livers
2 medium apples
½ cup dry sherry wine
  salt and pepper to taste
4 hard-boiled eggs

Chop the onion and sauté in butter until soft. Do not brown. Mix in the chicken livers. Core and slice the *unpeeled* apples and add to pan. Pour in the sherry and cook until the liquid is reduced by ½. Season with salt and pepper. Add eggs and work the mixture through the fine blade of a food chopper until smooth.

Pack the pâté into small decorative crocks and pour a layer of melted butter over the top. Cover securely and refrigerate or freeze. Serve with party rye or melba toast. Yield: 2 cups.

TUNA PÂTÉ

1 7-oz. can tuna, shredded
½ can small shrimp, mashed
6 slices cooked, crisp bacon, crumbled
¼ cup minced fresh mushrooms
3 tbsp. mayonnaise
3 tbsp. sour cream
2 tsp. lemon juice
¼ tsp. salt
  few drops of Tabasco sauce

Combine ingredients and mix until well blended. Pâté may be frozen in sealed plastic container. Use a fish mold if possible. Rub mold with mayonnaise and pack pâté into it. Securely wrap in foil and freeze. To serve: defrost gradually in refrigerator and unmold. Garnish with capers for eyes and pimiento for mouth. Serve with bland crackers. Yield: 1½-2 cups.

****Mild fish taste.

PINEAPPLE PÂTÉ
(Chicken Livers)

2 cups (1 lb.) butter, softened
2 lbs. chicken livers
2 chopped medium onions
1 tsp. curry powder
1 tsp. paprika
¼ tsp. salt
¼ tsp. freshly ground black pepper
3 tbsp. Cognac
1¼ cups sliced pimiento olives
1 top of fresh pineapple

Melt ½ cup butter in saucepan. Add chicken livers, onions, curry powder, paprika, salt and pepper. Cover and cook until livers are no longer pink (about 8 minutes). Blend the mixture little by little in an electric blender until smooth. Soften the remaining 1½ cups butter to room temperature and, using a spoon, thoroughly blend butter, liver mixture and Cognac.

Chill in refrigerator for at least 3 hours or until mixture may be molded. Mold into a pineapple shape. Starting at the base of the molded mixture, press the sliced olives in rows encircling the pâté so that it is completely covered except for the very top. Cap with top of pineapple. Voila! Pineapple Pâté.

To freeze: wrap entire mold in plastic wrap and then foil and seal securely. To serve: remove 24 hours before serving and defrost in refrigerator. This makes enough to serve 40 people at a cocktail party. Yield: about 5 cups.

****Absolutely spectacular — very little effort.

TAPENADE

 1 7-oz. can tuna with oil
 1 6-oz. tin anchovy fillets with oil
 ¼ cup capers
 18 pitted black Greek olives
    juice of 1 large lemon
 2 tsp. garlic juice
 ½ cup olive oil
 3 tbsp. Cognac
    freshly ground pepper to taste

Place first 6 ingredients in blender and blend at medium speed for about 3-5 minutes. Stop the blender occasionally to stir the mixture. Gradually add ½ cup olive oil. When all the oil has been added, the mixture should be the same consistency as mayonnaise. Blend in 3 tablespoons Cognac and the freshly ground pepper. To freeze: place either in a container and seal securely or in a decorative mold and wrap carefully in foil. To serve: defrost overnight in refrigerator and serve with thick black bread. Yield: 2 cups.

****For real fish lovers.

STORABLES

No need to look in the dictionary; "storables" is *our* word, not Webster's. It describes those foods which can be preserved in various pickling marinades and stored in the refrigerator for several weeks or more. These recipes are extras to supplement a large selection of hors d'oeuvre at a cocktail party or serve as a special dish before a dinner party.

Storables can be prepared easily at a convenient moment and refrigerated. In addition to entertainment fare, these recipes add special loving care to family dinners and, best of all, they make perfect hostess gifts.

The 8-oz. jar is a good size for gift giving. Sterilize jars in the dishwasher. Place vegetables in jar and pour in boiling liquid marinade. Seal with melted paraffin if they are to be stored for more than 2 weeks. Otherwise, cap the jars securely. Place them in refrigerator and serve whenever you want to add a taste treat to your meal or a different dish to the hors d'oeuvre tray.

MARINATED MUSHROOMS

1 lb. small fresh mushrooms
white wine
olive oil
1 tbsp. minced onion
1 tbsp. minced chives
1 tbsp. minced parsley
1 bay leaf
3 cloves
1 tbsp. pepper
dash of Tabasco sauce
½ clove of garlic

Wash mushrooms. (If they are large ones, halve or quarter each. Place in a jar and cover with wine. Let stand 2 hours and then drain. Place mushrooms back in jar and cover with olive oil and seasonings. Allow mushrooms to stand for at least 2 days to absorb seasonings. Serve with toothpicks.

CRISPY CARROTS

1 tbsp. chopped onion
3 minced cloves of garlic
3 tbsp. salad oil
1 lb. carrots
¼ cup vinegar
1½ tsp. salt
pepper to taste
½ tsp. dry mustard
1 tbsp. pickling spice
1 small onion, sliced in rings

Sauté chopped onion and minced garlic in oil for about 5 minutes. Scrape carrots and cut into strips about 3″ long and add to pan. Stir the vinegar, salt, pepper and mustard into the oil. Wrap the pickling spice in a small cheesecloth bag and add to the carrots. Cover and simmer for 5 minutes. Remove pickling spice. To store: place in plastic container with sliced onion rings on top and seal securely. Keeps 2 weeks.

CHICK PEAS

2 (1-lb. 4-oz.) cans chick peas, rinsed and drained
⅓ cup minced pimientos

Marinade

1⅔ cup white vinegar
¼ cup sugar
3 crushed cloves of garlic
1 tsp. grated lemon peel
2 tbsp. dried parsley flakes

Combine chick peas with pimientos and place in 5 (8-oz.) jars. Prepare marinade by placing all ingredients in saucepan and bring to a boil. Pour boiling liquid into each jar to cover. Cap securely and refrigerate. To store more than 2 weeks, seal jars with melted paraffin.

HEARTS OF ARTICHOKES

2 10-oz. pkg. frozen artichoke hearts

Marinade

1 cup salad oil
¼ cup lemon juice
½ cup lime juice
3 crushed cloves of garlic
2 twists lemon peel
2 twists lime peel

Cook the artichoke hearts according to package instructions. Drain and cool slightly. Place salad oil, lemon juice, lime juice, and garlic cloves in saucepan and boil. Using 2 (8-oz.) jars, place a lemon and lime twist into each jar and pack with cooked artichoke hearts. Pour boiling liquid over hearts. Cap securely and refrigerate. To store more than 2 weeks, seal jars with melted paraffin.

CEREAL CRISPS

⅔ cup melted butter
1½ tsp. celery seed
1½ tsp. garlic salt
6 cups small crisp cereal (Kix, Rice Checks, Stax, Cheerios)
2 cups stick pretzels
1 cup nuts (peanuts or mixed salted nuts — roasted)

Melt the butter in a small pan and add seasonings. Place the cereals, pretzels and nuts in a large flat pan. Sprinkle seasoned butter over cereal mixture and stir to blend. Bake in 250° oven for about 20 minutes. This can be stored in tightly sealed coffee cans in the cupboard for a month. Yield: 3 1-lb. cans.

****Nibble food.

PICKLED OKRA

4 10-oz. pkg. frozen whole okra
12 pickled red peppers, drained

Marinade

1 cup white vinegar
½ cup sugar
1 tbsp. chili powder
1 tsp. salt

Cook the frozen okra according to package directions until barely tender. Drain thoroughly. Place into 4 (8-oz.) jars, placing 3 pickled red peppers into each jar. Prepare marinade by combining all the ingredients in a saucepan and bringing to a boil. Pour the boiling liquid over the okra and peppers to cover. Cap securely and refrigerate. To store more than 2 weeks, seal the jars with melted paraffin.

DILL GREEN BEANS

¾ lb. green beans
⅓ cup red wine vinegar
½ tsp. crumbled dill weed
3 tbsp. olive oil
1 tsp. herb seasoning
1 tbsp. instant toasted onion

Just barely cook beans. Drain. Pour heated vinegar over the cooled beans. Add the rest of the ingredients (except onion) and toss to combine. Store in sealed container in refrigerator. To serve: sprinkle with the instant toasted onion.

SPICED CELERY

1 large bunch celery
1 green pepper
1½ tsp. salt
3 bay leaves

Marinade

1 cup cider vinegar
1 cup sugar
½ cup water
1 tsp. salt
1 tsp. ground ginger
1 tsp. ground allspice
¼ tsp. pepper

Separate celery into stalks and cut lengthwise to fit an 8-oz. jar. Cut pepper into 6 rings and place celery and pepper rings in saucepan with salted water to cover. Cover and simmer until barely tender. Drain and cool slightly. Pack into 3 (8-oz.) jars, putting 2 pepper rings around each bundle of celery and a bay leaf in each jar.

Make marinade by combining all ingredients in saucepan and bring to a boil. Pour the boiling marinade over celery and pepper to the top of jar. Cap securely and refrigerate. To store more than 2 weeks, seal jars with melted paraffin.

CHILI NUTS

1 lb. blanched almonds
3 tbsp. butter
2 tsp. chili powder

Brown the nuts in butter. Turn on to paper towels to drain. While still warm, sprinkle with chili powder. To store: put in air-tight can or jar. These nuts will stay crisp 2 weeks or more.

GARLIC OLIVES

1 jar (3-oz. pitted, green olives or a combination of pitted green and ripe olives
2 tsp. chopped parsley
1 crushed clove garlic
1½ tsp. olive oil
   salt and pepper to taste

Mix the first four ingredients together and gently toss to cover olives. Refrigerate 2 days before serving to combine flavors. Olives may be stored in a screw-top jar for several weeks.

MARINATED ARTICHOKES

1 large can artichokes
½ cup olive oil
¼ cup wine vinegar
¼ tsp. salt
¼ tsp. sugar
1 minced clove of garlic

Place all ingredients in a jar with a tight fitting cover. Shake well and let stand for at least 3 hours, inverting the jar several times to be sure it is well mixed. This marinade will keep in refrigerator for 2 weeks. To serve: drain and serve with toothpicks. These artichokes are also very good in a salad.

SPICED APRICOTS

1 pkg. dried apricots
2 tbsp. brown sugar
½ tsp. pumpkin pie spice
1 tbsp. white wine vinegar

Cook apricots according to package directions until almost tender. Allow for a cup of apricot syrup and add brown sugar, pumpkin spice, and vinegar. Simmer with apricots for 15 minutes. Store in sealed container in refrigerator. Serve hot or cold with toothpicks.

PICKLED CAULIFLOWER

1 small head cauliflower
1½ tsp. salt
1 3½-oz. jar pickled pearl onions, drained
1 jar miniature sweet gherkins, drained

Marinade
1¾ cups water
1½ cups tarragon vinegar
2 tbsp. sugar
1¼ tbsp. prepared mustard
2 crushed cloves of garlic
1 tsp. salt
pepper to taste

Break the cauliflower head into small flowerets. Cook in boiling salted water to cover until barely tender. They should still be slightly crunchy. Drain and cool. Pack about 6 (8-oz.) jars alternating with cauliflower, onion and gherkins.

Prepare marinade by combining all ingredients in saucepan and bringing to a boil. Pour over the cauliflower to cover. Cap securely and refrigerate. To store more than 2 weeks, seal jars with melted paraffin.

GENERAL HORS D'OEUVRE SELECTION

A selection of hors d'oeuvre is inescapable for the hostess. It does not matter whether she is giving a large cocktail party, an intimate dinner, or just having some neighbors in for drinks.

The original French tradition of hors d'oeuvre was food served outside the main meal or work. "Hors" is the French word for outside and "oeuvre" means work. The French hors d'oeuvre was an elegant first course prepared to excite the palate for the meal to come.

This custom has long since been Americanized. An hors d'oeuvre in today's vernacular is any "finger food" served as accompaniment to cocktails. Everything — from peanuts and pretzels to pâtés and pastries — is acceptably defined as hors d'oeuvre.

What to serve depends on the number of guests, facilities for serving, and the kinds of foods desired. Basically, all foods should compliment each other as well as the dinner, if it is to follow. Select by opposites: sweet and sour, hot and cold, mild and spicy, smooth and crunchy, light and heavy. If the entrée is rich, elaborate food, the hors d'oeuvre should be light and flavorful. The purpose is to stimulate the appetite not satisfy it. Allow for a minimum of 5 hors d'oeuvre per guest.

Garnish and decorate the bowls and platters with artistic flair. Guests appreciate the extra effort of a hostess. YOUR SECRET SERVANT gives you extra time for this extra effort.

CHEESE CHUTNEY BALLS

2 8-oz. pkg. cream cheese, softened
1¼ tbsp. minced onion (more if desired)
3 tbsp. finely chopped Chut-Nut
   salt and pepper to taste
1 3¼-oz. pkg. almonds, chopped and toasted

Thoroughly combine all ingredients except almonds. Make bite-sized balls out of mixture. Lightly toast chopped almonds in warm oven. Roll cheese balls in toasted, chopped almonds. Freeze uncovered on trays. Transfer frozen balls to plastic bag for freezer storage.

To serve: spread balls on tray and defrost 2 hours at room temperature or overnight in refrigerator. Yield: about 48 balls.

****Effortless!

CURRIED COCONUT BITES

1 3½-oz. can coconut
1½ tsp. curry powder
2 8-oz. pkg. cream cheese, softened
1 ounce sherry wine

Toast coconut and curry in 350° oven. Watch carefully because coconut burns easily. Combine cheese and sherry and make bite-sized balls of the mixture. Roll in the toasted coconut. Freeze uncovered on a tray. Transfer frozen balls to a plastic bag for freezer storage. To serve: spread frozen bites on a tray and defrost at least 2 hours in refrigerator. Serve cold. Yield: 48 bites.

****Quick and easy for a large crowd.

CARAWAY CHEESE BALLS

1 12-oz. container *dry* pot cheese
1 egg
2 tbsp. caraway seeds
1½ tbsp. sugar
4 tbsp. melted butter
pretzel sticks

Thoroughly combine all ingredients and shape into bite-sized balls. Bake in 350° oven for 20 minutes. Freeze uncovered on tray. Transfer frozen balls to plastic bag for freezer storage. To serve: spread frozen balls on tray and heat at 350° for 5-10 minutes. Use pretzel sticks as toothpicks. Yield: about 28 balls.

****Deliciously different.

SARDINE CHEESE BALLS

2 3¾-oz. can sardines, mashed
1 8-oz. pkg. cream cheese, softened
2 tsp. Worcestershire sauce
  salt and pepper to taste
1 cup finely chopped walnuts

Thoroughly combine all ingredients except the nuts. Make into bite-sized balls and roll each in the walnuts. Freeze uncovered on tray. Place frozen balls in plastic bag for freezer storage. To serve: spread frozen balls on tray and defrost for 2 hours at room temperature or overnight in refrigerator. Yield: about 32 balls.

BLUE CHEESE BALLS

1 8-oz. pkg. cream cheese, softened
2 ounces blue cheese
1 4-oz. can deviled ham
  onion powder to taste
1 cup chopped almonds
1 tbsp. butter
  pretzel sticks

Thoroughly combine cheeses, ham, and onion powder. Make bite-sized balls. Lightly sauté the chopped almonds in butter. Roll the cheese balls in the sautéed almonds. Freeze uncovered on a tray. Frozen balls may be transferred to plastic bag for freezer storage. To serve: separate frozen balls on flat surface and defrost 2 hours at room temperature or overnight in refrigerator. Use pretzel sticks as toothpicks. Yield: about 32 balls.

SHREDDED WHEAT CHEESE COOKIES

½ lb. processed grated American Cheese
⅓ cup butter, softened
¾ cup sifted flour
⅛ tsp. cayenne pepper
3 Shredded Wheat biscuits (finely crumbled)

Thoroughly blend cheese and butter. Gradually add flour, pepper and Shredded Wheat crumbs. Shape into ¾" diameter balls. Place on cookie sheet and flatten with a fork. Freeze uncovered on a tray. Transfer frozen cookies to a plastic bag for freezer storage. To serve: bake frozen cookies for 10-12 minutes. Yield: 48 cookies.

****Good and crunchy.

STUFFED EDAM

1 medium Gouda or Edam cheese (about 2 lbs.)
1 tbsp. onion juice
   prepared smokey mustard
1 tbsp. light cream

Have cheese at room temperature. Neatly cut off top of cheese and carefully scoop out the center, making sure the sides are thick enough not to buckle. Notch the edge of the cheese shell with a sharp knife, to give a jagged tooth effect. Mash the cheese with a fork while adding onion juice and mustard to your own taste. Mix in enough light cream to make cheese easily spreadable. Put cheese back in shell and freeze. Defrost in refrigerator 24 hours before serving. Decorate top with sprig of parsley. Serve with assorted crackers or party rye bread.

****Easy and festive.

FRENCH BREAD ROLLS

½ lb. grated Swiss cheese
½ lb. butter, softened
   light cream
½ cup Swiss cheese cubes, cut very small
¼ cup chopped chives
4 hard French rolls

Mix grated Swiss cheese and butter and add enough cream to make a thick paste. Blend in the Swiss cheese cubes and chives. Cut the ends off the hard rolls and remove center. Firmly pack each roll with the cheese mixture. Wrap securely in foil and freeze. To serve: defrost in refrigerator about 1 hour. Slice crosswise to serve in thin slices. Note: the filling can be almost anything on hand. Make sure the mixture is of cheese-like consistency. Yield: about 60 slices.

****A little goes a long way.

LIPTAUER CHEESE

1 16-oz. container creamed cottage cheese
4 3-oz. pkg. cream cheese, softened
½ cup butter, softened
1 2-oz. can anchovy fillets, drained and mashed
¼ cup chopped capers
2 tbsp. caraway seeds
2 tbsp. paprika
   pepper to taste

Blend the cottage cheese, cream cheese and butter together. Thoroughly combine this mixture with the rest of the ingredients. Place in sealed plastic container and refrigerate overnight to permit flavors to blend. Freeze. To serve: defrost overnight in refrigerator. Serve with plain crackers. Yield: about 3½ cups.

CHEESE BREAD CUBES

2 glass jars sharp cheddar cheese
1/4 lb. butter
3 tbsp. grated onion
1 tsp. Worcestershire sauce
1 beaten egg
1 loaf day-old French bread, crusts removed

Melt cheese and butter together and add onion, Worcestershire sauce and egg. Slice bread into 1" cubes and dip each cube into cheese mixture. Place on a large tray to freeze. Frozen cubes may be transferred to a plastic bag for freezer storage. To serve: place frozen cubes on tray and bake for 10-12 minutes in 350° oven. Serve piping hot with toothpicks. Yield: about 48 cubes.

****Simple — a cheese dream.

GINGER CHEESE BALL

1 8-oz. pkg. cream cheese, softened
1/4 cup ginger marmalade, slightly drained
1/4 cup crumbled almonds
1 tbsp. butter

Thoroughly combine cream cheese and ginger marmalade. Shape into ball and wrap in foil. Freeze. To serve: defrost 4 hours at room temperature or overnight in refrigerator. Reshape ball with hands. Lightly sauté crumbled almonds in butter. Roll the ball in the toasted almonds until coated. Serve with saltines or other bland crackers. Yield: about a 2 1/2" ball or 1 1/2 cups.

****"A taste of ginger."

CHEDDAR BEER CHEESE

½ lb. grated sharp cheddar cheese
½ clove of garlic, minced
6 drops of Tabasco sauce
1 tbsp. Worcestershire sauce
½ tsp. dry mustard
½ cup beer

Mix all ingredients until well blended. Pack in crocks or decorative pots. To store in refrigerator more than 2 weeks, seal with paraffin. To freeze: place in securely covered plastic containers and age in refrigerator for 3 days before freezing.

****A male favorite.

ROQUEFORT CHEESE SPREAD

¼ lb. Roquefort cheese, softened
1 8-oz. pkg. cream cheese, softened
¼ tsp. Worcestershire sauce
¼ tsp. garlic salt
¼ tsp. dry mustard
¼ tsp. curry powder
¼ cup sherry, Madeira or Port wine

Thoroughly combine all ingredients except the wine. Pack cheese in crocks or decorative pots. Make gashes in the cheese and pour in the wine. To store in refrigerator more than 2 weeks, seal with paraffin. To freeze: place in securely covered plastic containers and age in refrigerator for 3 days before freezing. Serve with plain crackers or water biscuits. Yield: 1½ cups.

CHILI-CHEESE LOG

⅓ lb. grated cheddar cheese
1 8-oz. pkg. cream cheese, softened
¾ cup chopped pecans
¼ cup chili powder

Thoroughly blend cheddar cheese and cream cheese. Mix in the chopped pecans. Shape mixture into a log. Lightly roll in chili powder and wrap securely in foil to freeze. To serve: defrost at least 4 hours at room temperature or overnight in refrigerator. Best served on warmed cocktail crackers. Yield: 2½ cups.

****Mild cheese mixture.

OLIVE-CHEESE LOG

¼ lb. blue cheese, softened
1 3-oz. pkg. cream cheese, softened
3 tbsp. butter, softened
3 tbsp. brandy or heavy flavored sherry wine
¾ cup minced pimiento olives
¾ cup chopped toasted almonds

Thoroughly blend all ingredients except the almonds, and form mixture into a log-like roll. Roll the log in the chopped, toasted almonds to lightly cover the cheese. Wrap in foil and freeze. To serve: defrost for 4 hours at room temperature or overnight in the refrigerator. Plain crackers go best with this roll. Yield: 2 cups.

****Pretty to serve.

HAM-OLIVE CHEESE LOG

    1 8-oz. pkg. cream cheese, softened
    1 4½-oz. can deviled ham
    ¾ cup minced pimiento olives
      minced parsley

Blend cheese, ham and olives. Shape into a log and roll in parsley. Wrap securely in foil and freeze. To serve: defrost for 3 hours at room temperature or overnight in refrigerator. Serve with plain wafers or crackers. Yield: 2 cups.

****Quick-as-a-wink specialty.

GERMAN POT CHEESE

    2 small (3-oz.) Camembert cheese
    1 Liederkranz (4 oz.) cheese
    ¼ lb. Roquefort cheese
    ¼ lb. cottage cheese
    ¼ lb. butter
    2 tbsp. flour
    1 pt. heavy cream
    1 cup minced pimiento olives *or*
    ¼ cup prepared bacon-bits
    ¼ tsp. cayenne pepper

Scrape the outside skin from the Camembert and Liederkranz cheeses. Place all the cheeses, butter, flour and cream in a pot and boil until melted, making sure to stir constantly. When the mixture is thoroughly melted, rub through a fine sieve or strainer. Stir in the minced olive *or* the bacon-bits and season with cayenne pepper. The bacon-bits give this cheese mixture a deliciously different taste.

Pack in decorative pots, seal and refrigerate or freeze. Each container should have a piece of wax paper over the cheese and be securely covered. The cheese keeps in the refrigerator for about 3 weeks. Yield: 3½ cups.

STUFFED KUMQUATS

1 jar preserved kumquats
2 3-oz. pkg. cream cheese, softened
2-3 tsp. crystallized ginger, minced
½ cup walnuts

Cut each kumquat in half. Mix together cream cheese and ginger. Spread each half. Garnish with a small piece of walnut. Wrap in foil and freeze. To serve: defrost for 3 hours at room temperature or overnight in refrigerator.

EGGPLANT PUFFS

1 medium eggplant
¾ cup grated cheddar cheese
1 beaten egg
¾ cup (dry) bread crumbs
¾ tsp. ground cumin seed
¾ tsp. garlic salt
2 tsp. lemon juice
  flour
  olive oil for frying

Peel eggplant and cut into small cubes. Place cubes in saucepan with enough water to barely cover them. Boil for 10-15 minutes or until tender. Mash the eggplant with a fork. Add grated cheese, egg, bread crumbs, and seasonings to the pulp. Blend thoroughly. Form the mixture into bite-sized balls. Chill at least 1 hour. Roll balls in flour and fry in ½" olive oil until crisp and brown.

To freeze: place uncovered on a tray. Transfer frozen puffs to a plastic bag for storage. To serve: place the frozen puffs on a cookie sheet. Bake in a 400° oven for 10-12 minutes until hot and crisp. Yield: about 60 puffs.

HAWAIIAN MEATBALLS

- 1 lb. ground beef, chuck or round
  salt and pepper to taste
- ½ tsp. onion or garlic salt
- 1 bottle commercial barbecue sauce
- 1 large jar small stuffed olives
- 1 large can pineapple chunks, halved

Season the meat with salt, pepper, and onion or garlic salt. Make bite-sized meatballs. Sauté meatballs in small amount of fat. Freeze in sealed container in barbecue sauce. You may substitute your own barbecue sauce or favorite sweet and sour sauce.

To serve: place sauce, meatballs, olives and pineapple chunks in chafing dish and heat until warmed through. Serve with large toothpicks for skewering meatballs, pineapple and olive together. Yield 42 meatballs.

****Exotic-looking South Sea fare!

SUCCULENT SPARERIBS

2 2½-lb. spareribs, cracked
1 lemon
  salt and pepper to taste

Rub finger-sized spareribs with salt, pepper and lemon. Separate them into finger pieces and place them in a shallow baking pan in a single layer. Bake at 350° for 1 hour.

Glaze with either a commercial barbecue sauce or one of the sauce recipes listed below. Baste frequently with selected sauce and cook an additional 45 minutes. Freeze spareribs (in the sauce) in a sealed container. To serve: defrost in refrigerator overnight and reheat in chafing dish. Yield: 30 spareribs.

Sweet and Sour Sauce

¾ cup sugar
2 tbsp. cornstarch
1 tsp. curry
⅛ tsp. ground cloves
¾ cup water
⅓ cup vinegar
2 tbsp. soy sauce
1 crushed clove of garlic

Mix sugar, cornstarch, curry and ground cloves. Slowly add water and stir until smooth. Add the remaining ingredients and heat well.

Currant Sauce

1 10-oz. jar currant jelly
1 cup ketchup

Combine and heat until jelly is melted.

****Good for cocktail buffet.

BOLOGNA WEDGIES

4 slices spiced bologna
2 3-oz. pkg. cream cheese, softened
¼ cup chives

Spread bologna with cream cheese, seasoned with chives. Place slices together as in a layer cake. Make sure you have a sufficient amount of cheese spread between the layers. Wrap securely in foil and freeze. To serve: defrost and cut in small wedges and spear each with a toothpick. Variations: use softened cream cheese and ¼ cup chili sauce. Yield: 12 wedges.

SURPRISE MEATBALLS

1 lb. ground round steak
1 well beaten egg
⅓ cup crushed corn flakes
⅓ cup milk
   garlic and onion salt to taste
   pitted ripe olives
   pitted green olives
   watermelon pickles
   sweet pickles
   cocktail onions.

Thoroughly combine all ingredients. Mold small bite-sized meatballs around pitted ripe or green olives, watermelon or sweet pickles or cocktail onions. Brown the meatballs in a small amount of butter. Freeze uncovered on a tray. Transfer frozen meatballs to plastic bag for freezer storage.

To serve: reheat in slow oven or lightly greased frying pan on low heat. The meatballs can be served with a mild barbecue sauce or several tablespoons of wine in the bottom of the chafing dish or other server. Serve hot with toothpicks. Yield: about 70 meatballs.

****New taste for an old standby.

DELUXE SWEDISH MEATBALLS

¼ cup milk
1 lb. ground chuck
¼ minced onion
1 slice bread, crumbled
1 egg
2 tbsp. chopped parsley
1 tsp. basil
2 tsp. grated lemon rind
2 tsp. lemon juice
  dash of nutmeg
  salt and pepper to taste
4 tbsp. butter
½ tsp. garlic salt

Soak bread in milk. Thoroughly combine all but the last 2 ingredients, and shape mixture into bite-sized balls. Brown in butter flavored with the garlic salt.

Sauce

3 tbsp. flour
½ cup beef bouillon
½ cup red wine
¾ cup sour cream

Make a gravy sauce by mixing flour with the beef bouillon until smooth. Heat and gradually add the red wine and sour cream. *Do not boil.* Add the meatballs to sauce and freeze in sealed plastic container.

To serve: defrost overnight in refrigerator and heat in chafing dish, being careful not to boil. Serve with toothpicks. Serving variations: meatballs may also be served in commercial barbecue sauce, undiluted tomato soup, spaghetti sauce or mushroom soup. Yield: 42 meatballs.

COCKTAIL CROQUETTES

A cocktail croquette is a prepared mixture of white sauce, meat or fish and special seasonings, which has been rolled into bite-sized croquettes and deep fat fried.

White Sauce

4 tbsp. butter
4 tbsp. flour
¼ tsp. salt
¾ cup heavy cream
¼ cup milk

For Frying

1 egg
bread crumbs
fat for frying

Make a white sauce by melting butter in saucepan over low flame or in top of double boiler and stir in flour and salt. Add cream and milk, stirring constantly until sauce is very thick. Select one of the following recipes and thoroughly stir the ingredients into the white sauce. Cool.

Shape the mixture into bite-sized croquettes. Dip them first into the beaten egg and then roll in bread crumbs. Fry in 1½″ of hot deep fat for 1-2 minutes until golden brown. Drain well on absorbent paper and cool.

To freeze: place uncovered on tray. Transfer frozen croquettes to plastic bag for freezer storage. To serve: place frozen croquettes on cookie sheet and heat in 400° oven for 20-25 minutes until thoroughly heated. Yield: about 36 croquettes.

Sauce for dipping (optional)

1 cup sour cream
½ cup minced ripe olives
1 tsp. crumbled dill weed
1 tbsp. lemon juice
2 tsp. minced onion

Thoroughly combine all ingredients.

1. Beef

    1 cup chopped roast beef
    2 tbsp. A_1 sauce
    1 tsp. dry mustard
    salt and pepper to taste

2. Chicken

    1½ cups minced chicken
    1 tsp. onion powder
    1 tbsp. chopped parsley
    salt and pepper to taste

3. Chipped Beef

    1 cup shredded dried beef
    1 tsp. A_1 sauce
    1 tsp. dry mustard

4. Crab, Lobster or Shrimp

    1½ cups shredded fish, cooked
    2 tbsp. chopped mushrooms
    ½ tsp. chopped tarragon
    1 tbsp. chopped parsley
    salt and pepper to taste

5. Ham

    1 cup chopped ham
    1 tsp. onion juice
    1½ tbsp. grated Swiss cheese

6. Salmon or Tuna

    1½ cups shredded fish
    1 tsp. minced onion
    ½ tsp. crumbled dill weed
    salt and pepper to taste

BACON SQUARES

6 slices bacon (thick cut is best)
1 beaten egg
  dash of Tabasco sauce
  dash Worcestershire sauce
  salt and pepper to taste
  bread crumbs
  fat for frying

Cut each slice of bacon into approximately 4 squares. Season egg with Tabasco, Worcestershire sauce, salt and pepper. Dip bacon in bread crumbs, egg, and back in bread crumbs. Fry in hot, deep fat. Drain thoroughly on absorbent paper and freeze uncovered on trays. Transfer frozen squares to a plastic bag for freezer storage. To serve: spread frozen squares on cookie sheet and heat in 400° oven for 10 minutes until crisp. Yield: 24 pieces.

****Unusual and easy.

CHEESE MEATBALLS

¼ lb. Roquefort or blue cheese
2 tbsp. Worcestershire sauce
¼ cup sour cream
1 tbsp. milk
1 beaten egg
1 tsp. salt
  dash of pepper
  dash of cayenne pepper
1 lb. lean chuck or round beef

Mix the cheese, Worcestershire and sour cream into a paste. Add the rest of ingredients and thoroughly mix them together. Make bite-sized balls. Brown meatballs in butter until just done. Freeze uncovered on tray. Transfer frozen meatballs to plastic bag for freezer storage. To serve: defrost 1 hour and reheat in a lightly greased frying pan or in slow oven. Serve hot on toothpicks. Yield: about 45 meatballs.

****Unusual.

FRANKFURTERS IN SOUR CREAM

1 lb. pkg. frankfurters
2 tbsp. butter
1 tbsp. flour
3 tbsp. chili sauce
1 tbsp. prepared mustard
2 tsp. sugar
1/4 tsp. salt
1 1/2 tbsp. caraway seed
3 cups sour cream

Cut each frankfurter crosswise into 7 pieces. Brown pieces in a little butter. Combine other ingredients and pour over frankfurters. Freeze in sealed plastic container. To serve: defrost 1 hour. Heat very slowly in a saucepan. Do *not* allow sour cream to boil. Transfer to a chafing dish with low heat and serve with toothpicks. Yield: about 70 pieces.

PORK MEATBALLS

1 lb. finely ground pork
1/2 cup minced onions
1/2 cup minced water chestnuts
1 1/4 tsp. salt
1/4 tsp. white pepper
2 eggs
1/4 cup flour
fat for frying

Mix chopped pork, onions, chestnuts, 1/4 *teaspoon* of salt and the pepper together. Chill the meat mixture for 30 minutes. Mix 1 teaspoon salt, egg and flour together to make a batter. Make small bite-sized meatballs, and dip them in batter and deep fat fry for 10 minutes or until there is no pink meat in center. Drain on absorbent paper. Freeze uncovered on tray. Transfer frozen meatballs to plastic bag for freezer storage.

To serve: heat in chafing dish. Serve with fancy toothpicks and a good sweet and sour sauce for dipping. (see recipe for "Succulent Spareribs") Yield: 42 meatballs.

CURRANT FRANKFURTERS

1 pkg. frankfurters
2 tbsp. butter
1 10-oz. jar currant jelly
1 cup ketchup.

Cut frankfurters into 5 bite-sized pieces each. Sauté in butter until just golden. Heat jelly and ketchup together until thoroughly melted. Combine with frankfurters and freeze in plastic container. To serve: heat in chafing dish and serve with toothpicks. Yield: 50 frankfurters.

****Inexpensive for a large crowd.

HAM MEATBALLS

1 lb. ground smoked ham
1½ lb. ground lean pork
¼ cup milk
1 slightly beaten egg
1 cup light brown sugar, firmly packed
½ cup white vinegar
½ cup water
½ tsp. dry mustard

Preheat oven to 350°. Thoroughly mix the ground ham, pork, milk and egg. Shape into bite-sized meatballs and place in a baking pan approximately 11" x 16". Mix together the brown sugar, vinegar, water and mustard to make a basting sauce and pour over the ham balls. Bake uncovered for about 1 hour. The ham balls should be basted several times while baking. Set aside to cool.

To freeze: place the meatballs and sauce in a container and seal securely. To serve: defrost just enough to remove the meatballs and sauce and place in chafing dish or similar server. Serve piping hot. Yield: 85 meatballs.

****Sugar glaze taste.

NORWEGIAN MEATBALLS

1 lb. ground round steak
½ lb. ground pork
½ cup dry bread crumbs
½ cup milk
1 egg
1 tsp. salt
¼ cup minced onion
1 tsp. sugar
2 tsp. powdered ginger
¼ tsp. nutmeg
¼ tsp. allspice

Gravy Sauce

¼ cup butter
1 tbsp. flour
1 cup milk

Thoroughly mix the ground meats together. Soak the bread crumbs in milk and combine with the meat. Mix in egg, salt, onion, sugar and the remaining spices. Shape into bite-sized balls and brown in a pan with a little butter.

In a separate pan make a sauce of the butter, flour and milk. Combine the meatballs and sauce in a baking dish and bake in 375° oven for about 1 hour. Set aside to cool. To freeze: place the sauce and meatballs in a container and seal securely. To serve: place directly in chafing dish or similar server. Heat the meatballs and serve piping hot. Yield: 60 meatballs.

CRABMEAT ALMOND BARS

    1   3-oz. pkg. cream cheese, softened
    2   tbsp. cream
    2   tbsp. chopped toasted almonds
    1   hard-cooked, chopped egg
    ⅓   cup flaked crabmeat
    2   tbsp. mayonnaise
    1   tsp. lemon juice
    ¼   tsp. celery salt
 9-12   white bread slices, crusts removed
        butter for spreading

Make 2 mixtures. First combine cream cheese, cream and toasted almonds. Then combine chopped egg, crabmeat, mayonnaise, lemon juice, and celery salt. Spread trimmed slices of bread with butter. Spread cheese and almond mixture on a second slice of bread. Lay first slice over it, buttered side up, and spread crabmeat mixture on this slice. Top with third slice, buttered side down. Gently press loaf together. Place on trays in layers. Wrap securely and freeze.

To serve: defrost and cut sandwich loaf in half lengthwise. Cut each lengthwise strip into 4 sections. Yield: 24-32 bars.

CRABMEAT SPREAD

    1¾ cup sour cream
    1¾ tsp. onion powder
     2 tsp. curry powder
     ½ tsp. salt
       dash of freshly ground black pepper
     3 drops of Tabasco sauce
     1 cup chopped, shredded coconut
     ½ lb. flaked crabmeat

Combine all ingredients thoroughly. Freeze in sealed plastic container. To serve: defrost overnight in refrigerator for several hours at room temperature. Serve with melba toast or crackers. Yield: approximately 4 cups.

****Coconut crabmeat delight.

CLAM BEIGNETS

     2 cans (7½ or 8-oz.) minced clams
     ½ cup butter
     ¼ tsp. salt
     ½ tsp. poultry seasoning
    1½ cups sifted flour
     4 eggs

Drain clams and preserve juice. Add water to clam juice to make a cup. In a saucepan combine liquid, butter, salt and poultry seasoning. Thoroughly stir in the flour and cook until the mixture thickens and begins to leave the sides of the pan. Beat in eggs, one at a time. Stir in the clams.

Drop the batter by the teaspoonful onto a greased cookie sheet. Bake in 375° oven for 12-15 minutes. To freeze: place beignets in plastic bag and seal securely. To serve: place on cookie sheet and warm quickly in hot oven. Yield: 60 beignets.

****Brings raves.

TUNA NUGGETS

2 7-oz. cans tuna fish
2 3-oz. pkg. cream cheese, softened
1 tbsp. lemon juice
2 tsp. horseradish
½ tsp. liquid hot pepper sauce
1 cup chopped parsley

Drain and flake tuna. Thoroughly mix cream cheese and tuna. Add lemon juice, horseradish, and hot pepper sauce. Mix thoroughly. Roll into bite-sized balls. Freeze uncovered on tray. Transfer frozen nuggets to plastic bag for freezer storage. To serve: separate nuggets on tray and defrost several hours at room temperature. Roll each nugget in chopped parsley. Yield: 40 nuggets.

PICKLED SHRIMP

1 sliced onion
1 sliced carrot
2 tbsp. chopped parsley
  small piece bay leaf
4 tbsp. lemon juice
2 cups dry white wine
  salt and pepper to taste
  dash of Tabasco sauce
2 lb. medium shrimp

Combine all ingredients but the shrimp and bring marinade to a boil. Simmer approximately 1 minute. Add shrimp and boil 3-6 minutes longer or until just cooked. Cool and freeze in marinade in sealed container.

To serve: defrost in refrigerator and serve either plain or with accompanying dip of Russian dressing. Use toothpicks for handling. Yield: about 150 shrimp.

COCONUT FRIED SHRIMP

- 1 lb. medium frozen raw shrimp
- ⅓ cup lemon juice
- ½ tsp. salt
- ⅓ tsp. ground ginger
- 3-4 tsp. curry powder
- 1¾ cups flour
- 2 tsp. baking powder
- 1¾ cups milk
- 1 3½-oz. can grated coconut
- fat for frying

Marinate shrimp in lemon juice, salt, ginger and curry for about 2 hours. Drain and reserve ¼ cup of marinade. Cut shrimp in 1″ pieces.

Prepare batter of 1⅓ cups flour, baking powder and milk and the ¼ cup of marinade. Toss *well-drained* shrimp into remaining flour; dip in batter and then in coconut. Fry 2 minutes in deep fat. Fry about 6 shrimp each time. Drain and cool shrimp. Freeze uncovered on tray. Transfer frozen shrimp to plastic bag for freezer storage. To serve: spread shrimp on cookie sheet and heat in 400° oven for about 7 minutes. Yield: about 125 pieces.

****Deliciously different.

SHRIMP AND RICE PUFFS

1 well beaten egg
½ cup tomato juice
1 cup cooked rice
½ cup dry bread crumbs
  pepper to taste
1 tsp. chopped parsley
½ tsp. celery salt
1 5-oz. can shrimp, drained and mashed
  fat for frying

Mix the egg and tomato juice and thoroughly blend in all other ingredients. Roll mixture into bite-sized balls. Drop into 1½" hot frying fat for 2-3 minutes or until golden brown. Drain on absorbent paper.

Freeze uncovered on tray. Transfer the frozen puffs to plastic bag for easier storage. To serve: place frozen puffs on cookie sheet and bake in 400° oven for 20-25 minutes until thoroughly heated. Yield: about 60 puffs.

LOBSTER CRISPS

1 7-oz. pkg. frozen lobster tails (1 cup
  cooked lobster meat)
1 boiled potato
2 tsp. grated onion
1 beaten egg
1 tsp. Worcestershire sauce
  salt and pepper to taste
  fat for frying

Remove lobster from shell and chop very fine. Peel potato and mince. Mix all ingredients together and roll into bite-sized balls. Fry in deep hot fat. Drain on absorbent paper. Freeze uncovered on tray. Transfer frozen crisps to plastic bag for freezer storage. To serve: spread frozen crisps on cookie sheet and bake in 400° oven for about 12 minutes. Yield: 18-20 crisps.

SHRIMP TERIYAKI

⅟₂ cup soy sauce
2 crushed cloves of garlic
½ tsp. dry mustard
2 tbsp. chili sauce
½ cup sherry wine
½ cup salad oil
1½ tbsp. sugar
2 tsp. red wine vinegar
1 tbsp. minced preserved ginger
2 lb. medium shrimp

Mix all ingredients except the shrimp in a pan and slowly bring to a boil. The shrimp should be cleaned and deveined. It is easier but more expensive to buy the shrimp already deveined. Place shrimp in shallow baking dish and pour the marinade over the shrimp and allow to stand for 2 hours.

To freeze: wrap securely in foil. To serve: remove the dish an hour or so before serving until the dish is nearly room temperature. Broil until shrimp are tender and slightly glazed, about 10 minutes. Baste frequently. Serve piping hot with toothpicks. Yield: about 150 shrimp.

****For shrimp lovers.

TUNA PUFFS

1 minced onion
  butter for sautéeing
3 tbsp. flour
3 tbsp. butter
¾-1 cup milk
1 13-oz. can tuna fish (or crabmeat), drained
¼ tsp. salt
⅛ tsp. pepper
½ cup flour
⅓ cup water
  dash of salt
2 stiffly beaten egg whites

Sauté onion in small amount of butter. Make a thick cream sauce with 3 tablespoons of butter, flour and the milk. Add tuna, onion, salt and pepper. Chill for several hours.

Make batter the consistency of a thin pancake batter, using ½ cup flour and ⅓ or more cup water. Add salt and fold in 2 beaten egg whites. Form bite-sized balls of tuna mixture. Use a slotted spoon and roll balls in the batter. Then, gently lower them into hot, deep fat and fry until puffy and brown. Drain on absorbent paper and freeze uncovered on trays. Transfer frozen puffs to plastic bag for freezer storage.

To serve: heat in 400° oven for 10-12 minutes. Yield: about 36 puffs.

****Extra special croquette.

SMOKED SALMON PASTRY ROLLS

Pastry

¼ lb. butter, softened
1 8-oz. pkg. cream cheese, softened
2 cups flour
2 tbsp. cold water

Cream butter and cheese together. Mix in flour with fingers or pastry blender, adding more if needed. Sprinkle water on dough and mix until it forms a ball. Divide pastry into two 9" circles.

Filling

½-¾ lb. smoked salmon, thinly sliced
½ cup minced scallion
black pepper, freshly grated
1 slightly beaten egg

Spread salmon evenly to cover pastry circles. Sprinkle with onion and pepper. Cut circle into 16 wedges and roll each wedge tightly from outer edge. Brush rolls with egg. Freeze uncovered on cookie sheet. Transfer frozen rolls to plastic bag for freezer storage. To serve: bake frozen rolls in 425° oven for 20 minutes or until browned. Yield: 32 rolls.

****Scrumptious.

CODFISH BALLS

1½ cups flaked codfish
2 cups instant mashed potatoes (whipped potato mix is easiest)
½ tbsp. butter or margarine
⅛ tsp. pepper
1 tsp. herb seasoning
1 slightly beaten egg
fat for frying

A package of frozen codfish may be used. Bake fish, as directed, until tender. Prepare mashed potatoes as directed. Thoroughly mix mashed potatoes, flaked cooked codfish, butter, pepper, herb seasoning and egg. Add salt if desired. Chill for 15 minutes and make bite-sized balls. Drop balls into hot frying fat and cook until brown. Drain on absorbent paper. To freeze: place in plastic bags and seal securely. To serve: heat the codfish balls in 425° oven for about 5-7 minutes. Serve on toothpicks with accompanying tartar sauce or tomato sauce. Yield 42 balls.

****Mild fish taste.

CRISP CURRIED SHRIMP

2 lb. medium fresh or frozen shrimp
1 cup dry bread crumbs
2 tsp. curry powder
½ tsp. salt
　　dash of pepper
1 tbsp. water
1 beaten egg
¼ cup melted butter

If shrimp are frozen, thaw to separate. Peel and devein. Combine crumbs, curry powder, salt and pepper. Add water to egg. Dip shrimp in egg, roll in seasoned bread crumbs and place on greased cookie sheet. Drip butter over shrimp. Bake 10 minutes at 375°. Freeze uncovered on trays. Transfer frozen shrimp to plastic bag for freezer storage.

To serve: spread shrimp on greased cookie sheet and bake for 5 minutes in 400° oven. Serve with orange sauce for dipping. Yield: 150 shrimp.

Orange Sauce

½ cup orange marmalade
¼ cup lemon juice
½ cup soy sauce
1 crushed clove of garlic
　　dash of powdered ginger
1 tsp. cornstarch
1 tbsp. water

Combine all ingredients except cornstarch. Heat while stirring constantly. Make paste of cornstarch and water. Stir in cornstarch paste. Set aside to cool and then freeze in sealed plastic container. To serve: heat in saucepan or small chafing dish. Yield: 1¼ cups.

****Savory shrimp.

ABBREVIATIONS USED

tsp.	teaspoon	oz.	ounce
tbsp.	tablespoon	°	degree
pt.	pint	lb.	pound
qt.	quart	pkg.	package or packages

CAN SIZES

6 oz. = ¾ cup   4½ oz. = ½ cup

8 oz. = 1 cup   16 oz. = 2 cups

EQUIVALENTS AND SUBSTITUTIONS

dash = less than ⅛ tsp.

1 tbsp. = 3 tsp.

4 tbsp. = ¼ cup

5⅓ tbsp. = ⅓ cup

8 tbsp. = ½ cup

2 tbsp. = ⅛ cup or 1 fluid oz.

16 fluid oz. = 1 pt.

1 cup = ½ pt. or 8 fluid oz.

4 sticks butter = 1 lb., or 2 cups

1 stick butter = ¼ lb. or ½ cup

1 lb. cheese = 5 cups fresh grated
  or 4 cups dry grated

1 lb. cottage cheese = 2 cups

8 oz. cream cheese = 1 cup

1 lemon, juiced = 2-3 tsp.

1 lb. all purpose flour = 4 cups sifted

3 oz. dried mushrooms = 1 lb. fresh

6 oz. canned mushrooms = 1 lb.

½ lb. raw mushrooms = 2½ cups

3 cups ground cooked meat = 1 lb.

¼-½ tsp. dried herbs = 1 tbsp. fresh

⅛ tsp. garlic powder = 1 small clove

INDEX

A

American cheese pastry, 41
  braids, 41
  cookies, 41
  cups, 42
  fillings for
    blue cheese, 42
    deviled ham, 42,61
    mushroom, 43
    shrimp, 43
    spicy beef, 44
    tuna, 42
  pinwheels, 42
  turnovers, 43
Anchovy roll-up, 15
Apricots, spiced, 77
Artichokes, hearts of, 73
Artichokes, marinated, 76
Asparagus and cheese roll-up, 16

B

Bacon biscuits, 57
Bacon wrap-ups, 21
Bacon squares, 95
Baked bean dip, 27
Baked bean canapé, 10
Beef croquette, 94
Blue cheese balls, 81
Blue cheese cookies, 46
Blue cheese dip, 28
Bologna wedgies, 91
Buckwheat dippers, 63
Butters, flavored
  caviar, 7
  chive, 8
  curry, 8
  herb wine, 8
  horseradish, 8
  mushroom, 9
  olive, 9
  Parmesan, 9
  poppy seed, 9
  sardine, 9
  shrimp, 9

C

Camembert biscuits, 57
Canapés

  baked bean, 10
  carrot, 3
  cheese-ham, 5
  cheese-pickle, 4
  chicken, 10
  chicken liver, 4
  corned beef, 11
  clam, 11
  crabmeat-horseradish, 4
  curried cheese, 5
  dill cheese, 19
  dried beef-cheese, 5
  ham-chutney, 12
  ham-pineapple, 12
  liverwurst, 6
  lobster, 18
  pimiento-anchovy, 6
  roast beef, 12
  Roquefort-sour cream, 7
  sardine, 13
  sardine-beet, 7
  shrimp toast, 14
  tuna, 13
  water chestnut-cream cheese, 13
Caraway cheese balls, 80
Carrot canapé, 3
Carrots, crispy, 72
Cauliflower, pickled, 77
Caviar butter, 7
Caviar dip, 30
Celery, spiced, 75
Cereal crisps, 74
Cheese

  asparagus and cheese roll-up, 16
  blue cheese balls, 81
  blue cheese cookies, 46
  blue cheese dip, 28
  blue cheese, pastry filling, 42
  bologna wedgies, 91
  Camembert biscuits, 57

caraway cheese balls, 80
cheddar dip, 35
cheddar beer cheese, 85
cheese and bacon wrap-up, 23
cheese biscuits, 62
cheese chutney balls, 79
cheese bread cubes, 84
cheese, crépe sticks, 50
cheese dip for meat, 35
cheese ham canapé, 5
cheese lamb dip, 27
cheese meatballs, 95
cheese-olive dip, 31
cheese pastry, American, 41
cheese pastry, cream, 40
cheese, filo filling, 54
cheese-pickle canapé, 4
cheese-shrimp dip, 34
cheese wafers, 46
chili cheese log, 86
chili-shrimp squares, 44
classic Roquefort dip, 27
crabmeat dip, 36
cream cheese pastry, 40
cumin seed wafers, 45
curried cheese canapé, 5
curried cheese cookies, 47
curried coconut bites, 80
dill cheese canapé, 19
dried beef cheese, 5
eggplant puffs, 88
French bread rolls, 83
German pot cheese, 87
ginger cheese ball, 84
ham-olive log, 87
hot clam dip, 33
hot ham dip, 33
Liptauer cheese, 83
nut-cheese dip, 31
olive cheese balls, 48
olive cheese log, 86
Oriental dip, 28
Parmesan butter, 9
Parmesan meringues, 63
quiches Lorraine tartlets, 60
Roquefort cheese spread, 85
Roquefort sour cream canapé, 7
salami cornucopias, 20
sardine cheese balls, 81

sesame seed wafers, 47
Shredded Wheat cookies, 82
shrimp Indienne, 29
spicy dip, 26
spinach and cheese filo filling, 55
stuffed Edam, 82
Swiss cheese fondue, 38
Swiss cheese puffs, 52

Cheddar beer cheese, 85
Cheddar dip, 35
Chick peas, 73
Chicken
    chicken canapé, 10
    chicken, crépes filling, 51
    chicken croquette, 94
    chicken liver-bacon canapé, 4
    chicken liver rumaki, 22
    liver pâté #1, 67
    liver pâté #2, 68
    pineapple pâté, 69
    rumaki, sweet sour, 21

Chive butter, 8
Chili cheese log, 86
Chili nuts, 76
Chipped beef croquette, 94
Chutney ham dip, 32
Clam beignets, 100
Clam canapé, 11
Clam dip, 31
Classic Roquefort dip, 27
Coconut fried shrimp, 102
Codfish balls, 107
Corned beef canapé, 11
Crab croquette, 94
Crabmeat almond bars, 99
Crabmeat horseradish canapé, 4
Crabmeat spread, 100
Crab, filo filling, 56
Cream cheese pastry, 40
    braids, 41
    cookies, 41
    cups, 42
    fillings for
        blue cheese, 42
        deviled ham, 42
        mushroom, 43
        shrimp, 43
        spicy beef, 44

tuna, 42
  pinwheels, 42
  turnovers, 43
Crêpes
  crêpes fillings, 50
    cheese sticks, 50
    chicken, 51
    newburg, 51
Crisp curried shrimp, 108
Crispy carrots, 72
Croquettes, 93
  beef, 94
  chicken, 94
  chipped beef, 94
  crab, 94
  ham, 94
  lobster, 94
  salmon, 94
  shrimp, 94
  tuna, 94
Crunchy dip, 28
Cumin seed wafers, 45
Cucumber ham dip, 32
Currant frankfurter, 97
Curry butter, 8
Curried coconut bites, 80
Curry, hot dip, 34
Curried cheese canapés, 5
Curried cheese cookies, 47

D

Deluxe Swedish meatballs, 92
Deviled ham pinwheels, 61
Deviled ham roll-up, 17
Dill cheese canapé, 19
Dips
  baked bean, 27
  blue cheese, 28
  caviar, 30
  cheddar, 35
  cheese-shrimp, 34
  cheese-lamb, 27
  cheese-olive, 31
  chutney-ham, 32
  clam, 31
  classic Roquefort, 27
  crabmeat, 36
  crunchy, 28

cucumber-ham, 32
dill dip, 37
eggplant Indienne, 36
french fried mushrooms, 37
guacamole, 30
hot clam, 33
hot curry, 34
hot ham, 33
nut-cheese, 31
oriental, 28
shrimp, 30
shrimp Indienne, 29
soy, 32
spicy, 26
smoked oyster, 29
Swiss cheese fondue, 38
tropical, 26
tuna, 29
Dried beef cheese canapé, 5

E

Eggplant Indienne, 36
Eggplant puffs, 88

F

Filo, 54
  filo filling
    cheese, 54
    crab, 56
    lamb, 55
    spinach and cheese, 55
Fish
  anchovy roll-ups, 15
  caviar butter, 7
  caviar dip, 30
  clam beignets, 100
  clam canapé, 11
  clam dip, 31
  coconut fried shrimp, 102
  codfish balls, 107
  crabmeat almond bar, 99
  crab croquette, 94
  crabmeat dip, 36
  crabmeat horseradish canapé, 4
  crab, filo filling, 56
  crabmeat spread, 100

crisp curried shrimp, 108
hot clam dip, 33
lobster canapé, 18
lobster croquette, 94
lobster crisp, 103
lobster roll-up, 18
newburg, crêpes filling, 51
pickled shrimp, 101
pimiento-anchovy canapé, 6
salmon croquette, 94
sardine butter, 9
sardine canapé, 13
sardine-beet canapé, 7
sardine cheese balls, 81
shrimp butter, 9
shrimp croquette, 94
shrimp pastry filling, 43
shrimp pâté, 66
shrimp and rice puffs, 103
shrimp teriyaki, 104
shrimp toast, 14
smoked oyster dip, 29
smoked salmon pastry rolls, 106
tapenade pâté, 70
tuna canapé, 13
tuna croquette, 94
tuna dip, 29
tuna nuggets, 101
tuna pastry filling, 42
tuna pâté, 68
tuna puffs, 105
Frankfurter-bacon roll-up, 22
Frankfurters, currant, 97
Frankfurter, sour cream, 96
French bread rolls, 83
French fried mushrooms, 37
Fritters, 53

G

German pot cheese, 87
Ginger cheese ball, 84
Green beans, dill, 75
Guacamole, 30

H

Ham
 cucumber ham dip, 32
 chutney ham dip, 32

deviled ham roll-up, 17
deviled ham pinwheels, 61
ham-chutney canapé, 12
ham croquette, 94
ham meatballs, 97
ham and mushroom roll-ups, 17
ham-olive log, 87
ham pineapple canapé, 12
hot ham dip, 33
 pickle and ham roll-up, 20
 pineapple ham roll-up, 20
 tropical dip, 26
Hawaiian meatballs, 89
Herb wine butter, 8
Horseradish butter, 8
Hot clam dip, 33
Hot curry dip, 34
Hot ham dip, 33

K

Kumquats, stuffed, 88

L

Lamb, filo filling, 55
Liptauer cheese, 83
Liver pâté #1, 67
Liver pâté #2, 68
Liverwurst canapé, 6
Lobster canapé, 18
Lobster croquette, 94
Lobster crisp, 103

M

Meat
 bacon biscuits, 57
 bacon wrap-up, 21
 bacon squares, 95
 bologna wedgies, 91
 cheese ham canapé, 5
 cheese lamb dip, 27
 cheese meatballs, 95
 chicken liver-bacon canapé, 4
 chutney-ham dip, 32
 corned beef canapé, 11

croquettes, 93
  beef, 94
  chicken, 94
  chipped beef, 94
  ham, 94
crunchy dip, 28
cucumber ham dip, 32
currant frankfurters, 97
deluxe Swedish meatballs, 92
deviled ham roll-ups, 17
deviled ham pinwheels, 61
ham-chutney canapé, 12
ham meatballs, 97
ham mushroom roll-ups, 17
ham-olive log, 87
ham pineapple canapé, 12
Hawaiian meatballs, 89
hot ham dip, 33
lamb, filo filling, 55
mock liver pâté, 66
pickle and ham roll-up, 20
pineapple and ham roll-up, 20
pork meatballs, 96
liverwurst canapé, 6
Norwegian meatballs, 98
roast beef canapé, 12
salami cornucopias, 20
sour cream frankfurters, 96
spicy beef pastry filling, 44
succulent spareribs, 90
surprise meatballs, 91
tropical dip, 26
Meatballs
  cheese meatballs, 95
  deluxe Swedish meatballs, 92
  ham meatballs, 97
  Hawaiian meatballs, 89
  Norwegian meatballs, 98
  pork meatballs, 96
  surprise meatballs, 91
Mock liver pâté, 66
Mushrooms
  french fried, 37
  marinated, 72
  mushroom butter, 9
  mushroom, turnover filling, 43
  mushroom roll-up, 16
  mushroom and ham roll-up, 17
  mushroom and nut roll-up, 18

N

Newburg, crêpes filling, 51
Norwegian meatballs, 98
Nut-cheese dip, 31
Nut-mushroom roll-up, 18

O

Okra, pickled, 74
Olive butter, 9
Olive cheese balls, 48
Olive-cheese log, 86
Olives, garlic, 76
Onion pizza, 58
Oriental dip, 28

P

Parmesan butter, 9
Parmesan meringues, 63
Parmesan wafers, 48
Party pizza, 59
Pastry
  bacon biscuits, 57
  blue cheese cookies, 46
  buckwheat dippers, 63
  Camembert biscuits, 57
  cheese biscuits, 62
  cheese pastry, 40
   American, 41
   cream cheese, 40
  cheese wafers, 46
  crêpes
  crêpes fillings, 50
   cheese sticks, 50
   chicken, 51
   newburg, 51
  cumin seed wafers, 45
  curried cheese cookies, 47
  deviled ham pinwheels, 61
  filo, 54
  filo filling
   cheese, 54
   crab, 56
   lamb, 55
   spinach and cheese, 55
  olive cheese balls, 48

onion pizza, 58
Parmesan meringues, 63
Parmesan wafers, 48
party pizza, 59
pastry filling
  blue cheese, 42
  deviled ham, 42
  mushroom, 43
  shrimp, 43
  spicy beef, 44
  tuna, 42
patty shell puff, 62
peanut butter braids, 45
pirozhski, 49
quiche Lorraine tartlets, 60
sesame seed wafers, 47
Shredded Wheat cookies, 82
smoked salmon pastry rolls, 106
Swiss cheese puffs, 52
Pâtés
  liver pâté #1, 67
  liver pâté #2, 68
  mock liver, 66
  pineapple, 69
  shrimp, 66
  tapenade, 70
  tuna, 68
Patty shell puffs, 62
Peanut butter wrap-up, 23
Peanut butter braids, 45
Pickle and ham roll-up, 20
Pickled okra, 74
Pickled shrimp, 101
Pimiento-anchovy canapé, 6
Pineapple and ham roll-up, 20
Pineapple pâté, 69
Pirozhski, 49
Pizza
  onion, 58
  party, 59
  presto, 19
Poppy seed butter, 9
Pork meatballs, 96
Presto pizza, 19

Q

Quiche Lorraine tartlets, 60

R

Roast beef canapé, 12
Roll-ups
  anchovy, 15
  asparagus and cheese, 16
  bacon, 21
  deviled ham, 17
  ham and mushroom, 17
  lobster, 18
  mushroom, 16
  nut-mushroom, 18
  pickle and ham, 20
  pineapple and ham, 20
  presto pizza, 19
  salami cornucopias, 20
Roquefort cheese spread, 85
Roquefort sour cream canapé, 7
Rumaki, sweet sour, 21

S

Salami cornucopias, 20
Salmon croquette, 94
Sardine canapé, 13
Sardine butter, 9
Sardine cheese balls, 81
Sesame seed wafers, 47
Shredded Wheat cookies, 82
Shrimp
  cheese-shrimp dip, 34
  coconut fried shrimp, 102
  chili-shrimp squares, 44
  crisp curried shrimp, 108
  pickled shrimp, 101
  shrimp and rice puffs, 103
  shrimp butter, 9
  shrimp croquette, 94
  shrimp dip, 30
  shrimp filling, turnovers, 43
  shrimp Indienne dip, 29
  shrimp pâté, 66
  shrimp Teriyaki, 104
  shrimp toast, 14
Smoked oyster dip, 29
Smoked salmon pastry rolls, 106
Soy dip, 32

Sour cream frankfurters, 96
Spiced apricots, 77
Spicy beef filling, turnovers, 44
Spicy dip, 26
Storables
    cereal crisps, 74
    cheddar beer cheese, 85
    chick peas, 73
    chili nuts, 76
    crispy carrots, 72
    dill green beans, 75
    garlic olives, 76
    hearts of artichokes, 73
    marinated artichokes, 76
    marinated mushrooms, 72
    pickled cauliflower, 77
    pickled okra, 74
    pickled shrimp, 101
    Roquefort cheese spread, 85
    spiced apricots, 77
    spiced celery, 75
    stuffed kumquats, 88
Stuffed Edam, 82
Stuffed kumquats, 88
Succulent spareribs, 90
Surprise meatballs, 91
Swiss cheese fondue, 38
Swiss cheese puffs, 52

T

Tapenade pâté, 70
Tropical dip, 26
Tuna canapé, 13
Tuna dip, 29
Tuna nuggets, 101
Tuna pâté, 68
Tuna puffs, 105
Turnovers, 43
    American cheese pastry, 41
    cream cheese pastry, 40
    fillings for
      mushroom, 43
      shrimp, 43
      spicy beef, 44

W

Water chestnut-cream cheese
    canapé, 13
Wrap-ups
    assorted bacon, 21
    cheese and bacon, 23
    chicken liver rumaki, 22
    dried fruit, 23
    frankfurter and bacon, 22
    peanut butter, 23
    sweet-sour rumaki, 21